Rethinking Economics

Economics is a broad and diverse discipline, but most economics textbooks only cover one way of thinking about the economy. This book provides an accessible introduction to nine different approaches to economics: from feminist to ecological and Marxist to behavioural. Each chapter is written by a leading expert in the field described and is intended to stand on its own as well as providing an ambitious survey that seeks to highlight the true diversity of economic thought.

Students of economics around the world have begun to demand a more open economics education. This book represents a first step in creating the materials needed to introduce new and diverse ideas into the static world of undergraduate economics. This book will provide context for undergraduate students by placing the mainstream of economic thought side by side with more heterodox schools. This is in keeping with the Rethinking Economics campaign which argues that students are better served when they are presented with a spectrum of economic ideas rather than just the dominant paradigm.

Rethinking Economics: An Introduction to Pluralist Economics is a great entry-level economics textbook for lecturers looking to introduce students to the broader range of ideas explored within the economics profession. It is also appropriate and accessible for people outside of academia who are interested in economics and economic theory.

Liliann Fischer has an International Relations background, recently graduating from her first Master's degree in Global Conflict and Peace Processes at the University of Aberdeen and is now studying for a second degree in Political Psychology at the University of Kent, UK.

Joe Hasell graduated in Philosophy, Politics and Economics (PPE) from the University of Oxford. Following a recent Masters in Economics and Finance at the University of Naples Federico II, Italy, he has just begun a PhD in Ecological Economics at the University of Leeds, UK.

J.Christopher Proctor studied Economics, History and Politics at the University of Tulsa before doing the EPOG Master's program at Kingston University, London and Université Paris 13. He is currently an Associate in Pluralist Economics for oikos International.

David Uwakwe became involved with Rethinking Economics while studying Political Economy at Kingston University, London. Since graduating, he has been working as a freelance journalist and is currently living in his native Dublin.

Zach Ward-Perkins is a former PPE student at the University of Manchester and a co-founder of the Post-Crash Economics society. Zach is one of the co-authors of *The Econocracy: The Perils of Leaving Economics to the Experts*.

Catriona Watson is a former PPE student, Head of Campaigns at Rethinking Economics and co-founder of the Post-Crash Economics society. She is now studying for a postgraduate degree in Economics at Leeds University, UK.

'The 2008 financial crisis and its continuing aftermaths have starkly revealed the limitations of the practice of intellectual "mono-cropping" in economics, that is, the near-total dominance by one approach to economics: Neo-classical economics. Leading the charge against this practice have been young economists from the Rethinking Economics movement. In this book, these young economists, rather than trying to replace one intellectual mono-cropping with another, provide a vision for a pluralist approach to economics. The volume, by presenting nine essays in which leading economists introduce the economic schools they represent, broadens our vision of economics and deepens our understanding of it. It is a highly relevant and enlightening contribution to a debate that will shape the future of the world economy as well as the way in which economics is taught and debated.'

Ha-Joon Chang, University of Cambridge, author of Economics: The User's Guide

'The members of Rethinking Economics haven't just protested against the narrowness of the conventional economics curriculum, they have done something about it. This volume admirably addresses their need for excellent up-to-date expert accounts of a range of different approaches to economics, all with student input.'

Sheila Dow, Emeritus Professor, University of Stirling, UK

'Economics students have been short-changed by degrees that teach only Neoclassical economics despite its failures before, during and after the crisis. This book provides a useful introduction to alternative voices in economics at a time when, though none of them has all the answers, they are each at least posing questions that the mainstream failed to even consider.'

Steve Keen, Kingston University London, UK

'This book is much more than a rethink of economics, it's a revolution in the economic landscape, democratizing theory and language for public benefit. This book builds a new corps of citizen economists and helps prevent economists-cum-pundits from pulling esoteric fast ones on the public. It's a must read for anyone wanting to challenge the economic system's dysfunctional status quo and an essential guide for advocates of social, economic and environmental sustainability. For genuine progress to occur, new economic theories, language and tools are needed. This book answers that call.'

Michael Shank, New York University, USA

'A timely and informative guide to competing schools of thought in economics. An excellent starting point for students looking for a broader economics education.'

Jo Michell, Senior Lecturer in Economics, UWE Bristol, UK

'"Is there life beyond mainstream economics?", you ask. Well, here is your answer: nine approaches, clearly explained by top specialists in each approach. This book produced by members of Rethinking Economics is warmly recommended.'

Victoria Chick, Emeritus Professor of Economics at University College London, UK

Rethinking Economics

An Introduction to Pluralist Economics

**Edited by
Liliann Fischer, Joe Hasell,
J.Christopher Proctor, David Uwakwe,
Zach Ward-Perkins, Catriona Watson**

LONDON AND NEW YORK

First published 2018
by Routledge
2 Park Square, Milton Park, Abingdon, Oxon, OX14 4RN

and by Routledge
711 Third Avenue, New York, NY 10017

Routledge is an imprint of the Taylor & Francis Group, an informa business

British Library Cataloguing-in-Publication Data
A catalogue record for this book is available from the British Library

Library of Congress Cataloging-in-Publication Data
Names: Proctor, J. Christopher, editor.
Title: Rethinking economics : an introduction to pluralist economics /
    edited by J. Christopher Proctor, Liliann Fischer, Joe Hasell,
    David Uwakwe, Zach Ward-Perkins, Catriona Watson.
Description: Abingdon, Oxon ; New York, NY : Routledge is an imprint
    of the Taylor & Francis Group, an Informa Business, [2017] |
    Includes bibliographical references and index.
Identifiers: LCCN 2017020044| ISBN 9781138222670 (hbk) |
    ISBN 9781138222687 (pbk) | ISBN 9781315407265 (ebk)
Subjects: LCSH: Schools of economics—Textbooks.
Classification: LCC HB75 .R4477 2017 | DDC 330.15—dc23
LC record available at https://lccn.loc.gov/2017020044

ISBN: 978-1-138-22267-0 (hbk)
ISBN: 978-1-138-22268-7 (pbk)
ISBN: 978-1-315-40726-5 (ebk)

Typeset in Bembo
by Apex CoVantage, LLC

Contents

Boxes and figures

Box

Figures

Contributor biographies

Post-Keynesian Economics

Engelbert Stockhammer is Professor of Economics at Kingston University London and coordinator of the Political Economy Research Group (PERG). He has worked on Post-Keynesian Economics, financialisation, wage-led demand regimes and economic policy in Europe and is ranked among the top 5% of economists worldwide by Research Papers in Economics (RePEc). He has published numerous articles in international peer-refereed journals, including the *Cambridge Journal of Economics, Oxford Review of Economic Policy, International Review of Applied Economics, Journal of Post Keynesian Economics, British Journal of Industrial Relations, Environment and Planning A*, and *New Political Economy*. Recent books include *Wage-Led Growth: An Equitable Strategy for Economic Recovery*.

Marxist Economics, Contributor 1

Ben Fine is Professor of Economics at the School of Oriental and African Studies (SOAS), University of London, holding honorary positions at the University of Johannesburg (Senior Research Fellow attached to the South African Research Chair in Social Change) and Rhodes University (Visiting Professor, Institute of Social and Economic Research). He is co-author with Alfredo Saad-Filho of *Marx's Capital* (sixth edition, Pluto, 2016), and chairs the International Initiative for Promoting Political Economy (iippe.org).

Marxist Economics, Contributor 2

Alfredo Saad-Filho is Professor of Political Economy at SOAS, University of London. He is co-author with Ben Fine of *Marx's Capital* (sixth edition, Pluto, 2016) and numerous other works on Marxist political economy, the political economy of development, neoliberalism, democracy, and alternative economic policies.

Austrian Economics, Contributor 1

Xavier Méra holds a PhD in economics from the University of Angers, France. He is a teaching and research assistant at Université Rennes 2 and an associated scholar of the

Ludwig von Mises Institute. His current research deals with the political economy of derivatives markets and monopoly theory.

Austrian Economics, Contributor 2

Guido Hülsmann is a professor of economics at the University of Angers and a Senior Fellow of the Ludwig von Mises Institute. His current research deals with money, banking, and the political economy of financial markets. More detailed information is available on his website: guidohulsmann.com.

Institutional Economics

Geoffrey M. Hodgson is a Research Professor at the University of Hertfordshire, UK. Among his publications are *Conceptualizing Capitalism* (2015, winner of the Schumpeter Prize), *From Pleasure Machines to Moral Communities* (2012), *The Evolution of Institutional Economics* (2004) and *How Economics Forgot History* (2001). He is Editor-in-Chief of the *Journal of Institutional Economics* and the Secretary of the World Interdisciplinary Network for Institutional Research (WINIR). He is a Fellow of the Academy of Social Science and the Royal Society of Arts.

Feminist Economics

Susan Himmelweit is emeritus professor of economics at the Open University. She is a feminist economist and an active member of the UK Women's Budget Group, a think tank that has monitored the gender impact of successive governments' social and economic policy decisions for more than twenty years.

Behavioral Economics

Stephen Young lectures at the University of Brighton Business School and the Brighton and Sussex Medical School, where he creates and delivers engaging interactive workshops for postgraduates from a wide range of backgrounds and disciplines. He also runs bespoke workshops for clients. He began teaching behavioural economics in 2009 in response to the failure of standard economics to explain the global financial crisis. Previously, Stephen worked in the public and private sectors, with a commercial background in the economics, strategy and regulation of global digital networks and services. An experienced conference speaker and author, he has worked as a consultant for clients including the United Nations International Telecommunication Union, and was previously Principal Analyst at ICT advisory firm, Ovum Ltd. Prior to that, he headed the public policy, public affairs and European Union regulatory functions at Europe's first full-service challenger telco, Mercury Communications Ltd. Website: www.stephen young.org.uk

Complexity Economics

Alan Kirman is Emeritus Professor of Economics at Aix-Marseille University and Director of Studies at the École des hautes études en sciences social es, Paris. He is a Fellow of the Econometric Society, has received the Humboldt Prize and has been a Member of the Institute for Advanced Studies at Princeton University. He is the author of 150 articles in international journals, and is author and editor of a number of books on Complexity Economics, most recently *Complexity Economics: Individual and Collective Rationality* (Routledge, 2010) and *Complexity and Evolution Toward a New Synthesis for Economics* (MIT Press, 2016).

Cooperative Economics

Molly Scott Cato is a Green Party member of the European Parliament for the South West of England and Gibraltar. She is also a Professor of Green Economics at the University of Roehampton and has published extensively in the fields of co-operative and green economics.

Ecological Economics, Contributor 1

Clive L. Spash is Professor of Public Policy and Governance, in the Department of Socio-Economics, Vienna University of Economics and Business, and editor-in-chief of the journal *Environmental Values*. He has published more than 150 academic journal articles and book chapters and most recently the 50-chapter edited volume *Routledge Handbook of Ecological Economics*. For further information, visit www.clivespash.org.

Ecological Economics, Contributor 2

Viviana Asara is Assistant Professor at the Institute for Multi-Level Governance and Development (Department of Socioeconomics) of the Vienna University of Economics and Business. Her research focuses on environmental politics and sociology, social movements and movement-parties, degrowth, ecological economics, political ecology, and democracy.

Acknowledgments

The idea for this book started at Kingston University London in the Autumn of 2014. Our professors actually came to us with the suggestion – the Rethinking Economics network had hosted dozens of lectures about different branches of economics. Why not turn some of those lectures into a book? At that time, there was no book on the market designed to introduce students to a wide range of economic theories. We could create that book.

From there, the project grew into the wider Rethinking network. Over a dozen Rethinkers contributed thoughtful comments in endless email chains about the nature and scope of the project, and helped build our list of academics to contact for contributions. Although there were too many helping hands to name, Yuan Yang, Matthew Wright, Jasmin Lukasz, Nicolò Fraccaroli, Ben Tippet, Maeve Cohen, Sam Wheldon-Bayes, Morven Oliver, Mark Restall, and Emma Hamilton were particularly helpful at this stage.

At the annual Post-Crash Manchester 'Unconference', we were introduced to John O'Neill, who knew just the publisher for this kind of book. We applied and were accepted by Routledge, and henceforth the long work of coordinating contributors, chasing up academic reviewers, and editing chapters began.

At this point the team had narrowed down to four core editors – Catriona Watson and Zach Ward-Perkins from Manchester and Dave Uwakwe and J.Christopher Proctor from Kingston. In the final months, we were joined by Joe Hasell and Liliann Fischer, who refreshed and energised us, helping carry the project to the finish line.

We would first like to sincerely thank our contributors. They graciously gave their time and expertise to this project, and showed a great deal of patience with the sometimes frustrating process of working with such a broad network of student-editors.

We also want to thank the many academics who helped review our chapters for content and the students – including Chris Harley, Julie Nelson, Holf Yuen, Karsten Köhler, Tom Winters, Michael Hamilton, Cahal Moran, and Gemma Wearing – who provided feedback on the early versions of our chapters.

This book would probably not exist without the leadership and work ethic of Will Horwitz, who did much of the coordination for the project in the first year. Professor Engelbert Stockhammer was also critical in kickstarting the project in its early days in Kingston.

Finally, we would like to thank everyone at Routledge for giving us this amazing opportunity. We are particularly thankful for Andy Humphries, the commissioning editor who encouraged us to put together a proposal for this book, and for our editorial assistant Laura Johnson, who showed us infinite patience as we learned just how much work it takes to make a book.

Parts of the introduction to this book appear in an article by J.Christopher Proctor in issue 9 of the Independent Social Research Foundation's *Bulletin*, and parts of the introduction and epilogue appear on Rethinking Economics' website and promotional materials. The explanation of 'neoclassical' economics in our introduction comes from '*The Econocracy*' by Rethinkers Cahal Moran, Joe Earle, and Zach Ward-Perkins.

Liliann Fischer (Aberdeen, Scotland)
Joe Hasell (Naples, Italy)
J.Christopher Proctor (Dallas, USA)
David Uwakwe (Dublin, Ireland)
Zach Ward-Perkins (Sheffield, England)
Catriona Watson (Manchester, England)

Foreword

Economics is a social science. It is neither a branch of mathematics nor the study of nature. It is, instead, analysis of humans by humans. This makes it both exceptionally important and extremely difficult.

Economics is important, because the way we understand how an economy both does and should work will, quite rightly, change how we do and should behave.

Economics is difficult, because it does not study a demarcated sphere of behaviour. What we consider to be economic behaviour is but a part of the totality of human action.

Psychologists, sociologists, anthropologists, geographers and historians also analyse the phenomena considered by economists. The assumption that it is possible to separate out economic behaviour and objectives from other forms of human behaviour and objectives is an heroic simplification and, like all such simplifications, it is fundamentally false.

This is not an argument against it. Simplification is often necessary if one is to make any progress in understanding. The neoclassical assumptions of individualistic utility-maximising behaviour and a calculable future are, for example, fruitful simplifications. They have often produced a better understanding of the behaviour we call 'economic'.

But the assumption of utility-maximisation is either tautological or untrue. Human beings are intensely social animals. The assumption that we are solipsistic egotists is false. Indeed, we consider such people to be psychopaths. Similarly, the assumption of a calculable future can be productive. But it, too, is false. The future is uncertain. We do not know what is going to happen.

The apparatus of neoclassical economics builds on shaky foundations. It violates norms of human behaviour. It is inconsistent with how humans actually behave. It does not even allow us to understand fully such important economic phenomena as bubbles and financial crises.

Therefore, we should confront the heterodox ideas and traditions represented in this book. The economics that humanity will need will surely display the vigour of the mongrel, not the neuroses of the pure-bred. It will build on a better understanding of what humans desire and how they behave. It will abandon the assumptions that the study of humanity is a lost branch of physics, humans are desiccated calculating machines, a separate sphere of economic behaviour exists and economic outcomes have nothing to do with power.

Consider the obvious: the political and social institutions that economists mostly ignore also have economic purposes. They are part of the economic world, just as the economic world is part of them.

I would not recommend an 'anything goes' approach. Economists need just enough complexity to achieve a reasonable understanding of what is going on, but not more. Simplification is a necessary part of the study of something as complex as human social behaviour. Otherwise, it will collapse into mere description.

At the same time, simplification can all too easily deliver falsehood. To avoid that trap, economists need to become aware of how the heterodox think. They need both to broaden their ideas and to show humility. As Hamlet would tell us, "there are more things in heaven and earth, economists, than are dreamt of in your philosophy".

I do not know how this journey will end, but I feel sure it is the right one. Neoclassical economics has become something very like a secular religion. The solution will not be its replacement by another such religion, but it will, among other things, demand that we pay attention to other traditions of thought. Read and learn: it may be painful, but it will be salutary.

Martin Wolf, Chief Economics Commentator,
Financial Times, London

Introduction

Rethinking economics

For those of us born into an era that promised 'an end to boom and bust' and that 'the central problem of depression prevention had been solved', the economic events of 2008 and 2009 came as quite a shock. The global financial system had just collapsed. Hundreds of thousands of jobs were being lost each month. The biggest economic crisis since the Great Depression of the 1930s was on hand.

But in economics class? None of that. Each day, as the economy disintegrated, we would open our textbooks to gracefully shifting supply and demand curves and movements along production possibility frontiers. The models worked perfectly but had little to do with the economy we saw at home and in the news. Instead of being introduced to warring factions who were all trying to offer their own explanation of what went wrong and how best to fix it, economics was presented as a placid, settled subject, with physics-like laws that kept everything operating in perfect order. But if these experts had it all figured out, why on earth couldn't they stop the sky from falling?

It was an incredibly frustrating time to be an economics student. We'd gone to university hoping to get our heads around this global turmoil and to work out solutions to the greatest challenges of our time, but instead we were just ploughing through problem set after problem set. Around the world, university students channeled this frustration into attempts to invigorate and revitalize the subject of economics. We lobbied our departments for better curricula whilst organising our own debates, reading groups and conferences. Out of these local campaigns grew Rethinking Economics, an international network of students who are campaigning for an economics education that is both open to new ideas and applicable to the real world.

In the meantime, we are educating ourselves in alternative ways to do economics that we can't find in our lectures and tutorials. We believe in being the change we want to see, so as students and recent alumni, we wanted to create the kind of book we wish we had been assigned in an Introductory Economics class – an introduction, if you will, to pluralist economics.

What is pluralist economics?

If you were to take an Introduction to Economics class, the entire class would probably be taught from one big textbook. You would study things like comparative advantage and aggregate supply and demand, learn to recreate some graphs and take a few multiple-choice tests. By the end there's a decent chance you would leave thinking economists pretty much had it all figured out.

If you took a few more economics classes, at some point you'd probably be told that there are some big fights in economics. Guys like Paul Krugman think markets make big mistakes and the government should intervene to help. Others, like the late Milton Friedman, are skeptical of the government and think markets are generally best left alone.

And if you stick it out and actually get a university degree in economics, at some point (if you're lucky) you might even get to learn a little history about Adam Smith's invisible hand, David Ricardo's ideas about trade, and the debates between John Maynard Keynes and Friedrich Hayek about how to respond to the horrors of economic depression.

All this might sound like a lot of disagreement, but it's actually just the tip of the iceberg of what economics has to offer. Economics is a hugely varied field, with an amazingly colourful array of different paradigms, methods and focuses, and pluralist economics is an education that includes all of these. Marxists have tools to analyse power relations and large historical trends and Post-Keynesians to deal with uncertainty, stagnation and crisis. Feminists bring gender into the equation and challenge our notions of what qualifies as work, while Institutionalists situate economics in historical time and space, filling in detail where other schools leave broad strokes. Austrian economists force us to consider the problems inherent with government power, while Behavioral economists probe the depths of human psychology to better understand how we make decisions. Complexity economists use cutting-edge mathematical tools to find patterns in the chaos of modern economies, and Cooperative economists work out bold and innovative new ways to organize production and consumption. Finally, Ecological economics offers a challenge to all schools of economic thought, insisting that human 'economic' activities be seen in a broader ecological context, one in which sustainability becomes not a buzzword but the central concern.

What gets included in introductory textbooks is just one branch of economics, sometimes called mainstream or neoclassical economics, which centers on analysing the world of markets and exchange. Throughout this book, many authors will make references to both 'mainstream' and 'neoclassical' economics, so it's worth taking a second to discuss the terms.

Neoclassical economics is a rich economic tradition that developed in the late 1800s out of the 'classical' tradition of economists like Adam Smith and David Ricardo (hence, the 'neo' classical). Neoclassical economics rests on three main conceptual pillars –

individualism, optimisation, and equilibrium – which are described in Box 1. Virtually all introductory economic textbooks are written from a neoclassical perspective, and neoclassical economics is often referred to simply as 'mainstream' economics.

Box 1: The three prongs of neoclassical economics

Individualism: Neoclassical theory focuses on the behaviour of individual agents, an 'agent' being defined as some sort of economic decision-maker. These include agents such as consumers, who must decide what to buy, but also entails modelling the production decisions of firms or even the political decisions of governments as individual decisions. Neoclassical economics therefore has an 'atomistic' view of the world, and tries to build an understanding of the economy as a whole from the decisions of individuals.

Optimisation: These agents seek to optimise explicit goals in their behaviour. The definition of 'optimise' is to "make the best or most effective use of a situation or resource". Consumers might want to use the money they have to buy the commodities they want the most; a firm might want to get the highest profit given the materials available and their technological prowess. The aims of agents can be wide ranging, and they may even suffer from faulty decision making, but in neoclassical economics, agents almost always optimise some goal.

Equilibrium: The decisions of individual agents must balance – a situation which is called 'equilibrium'. Agents make decisions about what to produce, buy, sell and invest in, and if these decisions are correct, then no agent will have an incentive to change its behaviour. Agents adjust their behaviour until they have, based on their individual judgment, achieved the outcome which is best for them, and there is no reason for anyone to alter their behaviour, resulting in a stable equilibrium.

"Earle, Moran, Ward-Perkins (2016) p 38. Based on (Varoufakis and Arnsperger 2006)."
This comes from *The Econocracy* http://www.manchesteruniversitypress.co.uk/9781526110138/

But 'mainstream' is actually a fairly loose term, as it just refers to the set of economic ideas that are most popular, or most dominant, at a given time. What's popular or accepted obviously changes over time – Keynesian economics, for instance, has come in and out of fashion over the years (more on that in our Post-Keynesian chapter). What is considered 'mainstream' also differs depending on which institutions you look at, because the academic world, policy world and financial world often embrace very different sets of economic ideas. Another word that gets used a lot in this book is 'heterodox', which simply refers to economic ideas that are not in the mainstream.

Neoclassical economics is one important branch of economics, but there are many more branches, which ask different questions and focus on different parts of the economy.

Our goal in creating this book is not to attack neoclassical economics or even to promote heterodox economics. Our goal is to promote 'pluralist' economics. Pluralism means embracing a broad tapestry of economic ideas, and a pluralist education is one that teaches prevailing theories but also introduces critical and dissenting ideas. A pluralist education gives students the tools to think critically about contrasting arguments and encourages them to ask new and important questions about the economy and their place within it. And we want to live in a world where this kind of critical, pluralist education is considered 'mainstream'.

About our introduction to pluralist economics

This book is designed to give anyone interested in economics a first step into the world of pluralism described above. The book was written by academics and experts in various fields of economics, and compiled and edited by a small team of students and recent graduates from Rethinking Economics. Each chapter was reviewed by a second academic. A larger number of Rethinking Economics students also provided feedback on individual chapters.

It should be noted that most of the schools of thought presented within this book are themselves subject to considerable internal differences and disagreements. All of our authors came to the project with a unique understanding of their own fields, and their chapters reflect this.

We are also very aware that this book shows only a fraction of the richness of economic thought that could possibly be included. As there is no shortage of introductory materials explaining neoclassical economics, we decided to omit it from this collection. We were also unable to include introductions for all of the fields of economics we would have liked to include, but intend to expand this book in future editions.

Finally, we want to stress that economists and the different branches of 'economics' do not have a monopoly on economic knowledge. Other social sciences like political science, sociology, anthropology and history, as well as other fields like the hard sciences, philosophy, psychology, literature and the arts, make meaningful contributions to our understanding of the economy and should be included in a fuller pluralist education. Each chapter of this book stands alone and does not have to be read in any particular order.

With this book we invite you to disagree, to doubt and dissent and to engage in an open debate about economics. No theory should ever become so accepted that it is no longer challenged, and healthy pluralism is always characterised by an open debate in which a multitude of different schools are invited to participate.

In this sense, this book is an uncomfortable book. We do not offer you the relaxing certainty of a universal truth that explains everything. On the contrary, we invite you to uncover glimpses of truth in a field characterised by fundamental uncertainty.

Rethinking economics for the 21st century

The financial crisis of 2008 is over, but its effects are not. Unemployment, stagnant wages and a general pessimism about the economy still dominate conversations around the world. Meanwhile, longstanding problems like climate change, food insecurity and high levels of inequality continue to fester.

The power of the discipline of economics to shape world history has long been recognised. Indeed, in the 1930s, John Maynard Keynes argued that the world was "ruled by little else". Economics matters. And for too long economics has been too narrow, both in the ideas it considers and the people it includes.

We hope that this book will enable the next generation of students and thinkers to embrace the discipline in its entirety – to encourage them to ask questions, question answers and dare to rethink economics.

<table>
<tr><td>1</td><td># Post-Keynesian economics

Engelbert Stockhammer</td></tr>
</table>

Post-Keynesian economics

Engelbert Stockhammer

Introduction

The publication of John Maynard Keynes' *General Theory of Employment, Money and Interest* in 1936 marked a turning point in the history of economic thought. It was written in response to the Great Depression and provided a theoretical framework for understanding financial crises and involuntary unemployment. Politically, this lent itself to a justification for government intervention and financial regulation: if capitalist market economies are unstable and prone to generate periods of high unemployment, governments should stabilise the economy by running budget deficits in times of crises and regulate finance to prevent the emergence of bubbles. This provided a reference point for the socially inclusive economic policy in the postwar era. During the 1980s, Keynesianism was abandoned and policy makers around the world switched to 'unleash capitalism', which resulted in the global financial crisis in 2008. Since then, Keynesian theory has met renewed interest.

In terms of economic theory, the Keynesian revolution has led to several very different responses. First, modern mainstream ('neoclassical') economics grew out of the rejection of Keynes and has resurrected orthodox 'supply-side' economics, which is generally hostile to government intervention. Second, some economists have tried to marry Keynes and neoclassical economics, which is often called the Neoclassical-Keynesian Synthesis. Third, it led to the development of Post-Keynesian Economics (PKE), a school of thought that highlights the distinctiveness of Keynes' approach. PKE takes Keynes' break from orthodox economics as its starting point, but it has on several issues gone beyond Keynes' own analysis. The Keynesian revolution, in the PKE view, did not go far enough. In particular, PKE has incorporated the analysis of class relations and developed further the role of income distribution and the theory of endogenous money and financial instability, as discussed below. Next to Keynes, Michał Kalecki, Joan Robinson, Nicholas Kaldor and Hyman Minsky have been important proponents within this vein.

The Post-Keynesian view of how capitalism works is in sharp contrast to the neoclassical view: capitalist market economies have weak self-stabilising mechanisms; they lead to involuntary unemployment and exhibit frequent crises. Theoretically, the most important feature of PKE for macroeconomic analysis is the principle of *effective demand*, which states that expenditures (or demand) will determine output (e.g. economic growth), as savings adjusts via the 'multiplier' process. PKE has developed a distinct growth theory and distinguishes between wage-led and profit-led demand regimes. It argues that (a) financial markets are prone to instability and will, if left on their own, lead to boom-bust cycles; (b) money is created by banks as a side effect of their lending decisions; (c) involuntary unemployment is a normal feature of labour markets; and (d) wage cuts and structural reforms cannot cure unemployment. This chapter will explain these building blocks and core theoretical arguments of PKE, after briefly touching upon its historical development.

Streams of Post-Keynesian Economics and differences to mainstream Keynesians

The term Post-Keynesian Economics was coined in the 1970s; however, the intellectual history of PKE is older than that. The first generation of Post-Keynesians – Joan Robinson, Nicholas Kaldor, Richard Kahn and Michał Kalecki – were mostly part of the Cambridge Circle, a group of economists who worked closely with Keynes at the University of Cambridge. To properly understand the development of PKE we first have to understand the changing reception of Keynesian arguments within the dominant economic schools of the day. Soon after the publication of the *General Theory*, there were attempts to marry neoclassical economics and Keynesian theory, which came to be known as the Neoclassical-Keynesian Synthesis. It was led by John Hicks (1937), who developed the 'IS-LM model', which was popularised by Paul Samuelson's widely used textbook and remains a mainstay of economics textbooks to this day. Ultimately the Synthesis tried to re-interpret Keynes as a special case of general equilibrium theory with wage and price 'rigidities'. The Synthesis approach created the division of economics into Macroeconomics, where Keynesian ideas played a prominent role, and Microeconomics, which was neoclassical terrain.

Within Macroeconomics the short-run/long-run distinction plays a key role in reconciling the Keynesian and classical elements. In the short run, the world works largely along Keynesian lines: demand determines output and involuntary unemployment is caused by lack of 'effective demand'. This is due to 'rigidities' like sticky prices and inflexible wages. Prices at restaurants are a common example – supply and demand might change constantly, but printing new menus is expensive so prices can stay 'stuck' for some time. However, in the long run, when prices and wages have time to adjust, the economy should function according to neoclassical theory. In the Synthesis, Keynes was reduced to a special case, if a practically important one, of general equilibrium theory.

In this period Post-Keynesians were mostly centred in Cambridge and criticised the Synthesis, or as Joan Robinson called them the 'bastard-Keynesians', for reducing Keynes to wage and price rigidities. Keynes did argue that wages were in fact inflexible, but as explained later, wage inflexibility is *not* the reason for unemployment.

In the 1950s and 60s PKE tried to generalise the short-term Keynesian analysis and develop an independent analysis of the long period and the distribution of income. The first-generation PK growth models have two distinct features. First, 'animal spirits' – capitalists' willingness to invest – play a key role as investment is an independent variable in the long run (as opposed to being determined by the rate of savings, as in neoclassical theory). Second, the distribution of income becomes a key adjusting variable, because wage and profit income are associated with different saving and spending rates, or 'marginal propensities to consume'. When someone spends money, it gets passed around the economy many times after the initial transaction. In this sense, new spending has both an initial effect on effective demand (from the original purchase) and a 'multiplier effect' from all the additional purchases made possible by passing around the original money. If workers spend a bigger portion of their income than capitalists, then wages should also have a higher 'multiplier' than profits, and increasing wages (even at the expense of profits) could be a way to increase effective demand. In this period PKEs also criticised the neoclassical 'marginal product theory' of income distribution as logically incoherent in the so-called Cambridge Capital Controversies.

In the 1970s mainstream economics changed, and by 1980 the so-called bastard-Keynesians found themselves outside of the new mainstream, as the new schools of 'Monetarism' and 'New Classical Economics' challenged even the watered-down parts of Keynesianism left in the Synthesis of the '50s and '60s. This was part of the rise of neoliberalism and resulted in a narrowing of the methods and theories acceptable in the economics profession. Macroeconomics now had to be derived from strict microfoundations based on optimising behaviour, and markets were assumed to clear. For critical economists life became more difficult.

That is why PKE (as well as other heterodox economics streams) began to institutionalise in the 1970s and '80s by setting up their own scholarly associations and academic journals – the established journals wouldn't publish their work anymore. This is the time when PK academic journals like the *Cambridge Journal of Economics* and the *Journal of Post Keynesian Economics* were founded. At the same time there was a geographical shift. When the first generation of PKs retired at Cambridge, they were replaced by mainstream economists. PKE lost its centre, but it gained breath; there were now PK traditions and networks in several countries, and the USA started to play a more prominent role.

With the political changes and the New Classical counterrevolution there was a new generation of PKs working on different topics. In response to Monetarism, the theory of 'endogenous money' was developed; the concept of 'fundamental uncertainty' was elaborated upon. In the 1980s there was also a shift to more short- to medium-term models; PKE developed the 'wage-led growth' models and there was more applied and policy-oriented work. Financial issues became more prominent.

The 1980s and '90s also saw a new version of mainstream Keynesians. The so-called New Keynesians accepted methodological individualism and the need for 'microfoundations' of macroeconomic models, but they argued that optimising behaviour does not necessarily imply market clearing and full employment. Thus were developed theories of 'rational wages' and 'price stickiness', based on transaction costs such as menu costs. This led to a New Synthesis model that again has a short-run/long-run dichotomy but is now based on rigid microfoundations. The Keynesian world is again a special case of the general equilibrium.

PKs are highly critical of the rational-behaviour microfoundations and have pointed out that the New Keynesian models have no independent role for investment expenditures and lack any meaningful role for finance. Macroeconomic models with a central role for income distribution have been refined by Post-Keynesians – building on the work of Michał Kalecki. The theories of endogenous money, financial instability and debt cycles have been developed – building on the work of Nicholas Kaldor and Hyman Minsky.

Today, the PKE paradigm is intellectually consolidated but academically marginalised. PKE is now a relatively coherent body of knowledge, with several textbooks, journals and scholarly societies in several countries. However, the streamlining of the discipline of economics, through journal ratings and, in the UK, the Research Excellence Framework, makes it ever more difficult to pursue an academic career as a Post-Keynesian or, for that matter, as any kind of heterodox economist.

The financial crisis of 2008 has shaken the trust of the public in the economics profession, but not dented the self-confidence of economic orthodoxy. It has inspired the interest of a new generation of critical students and, in many cases, also the broader public in PKE.

Foundations: uncertainty, social conflict and institutions

Modern mainstream economics is based on methodological individualism: the individual is the basic unit of analysis. Social and economic phenomena have to be explained from individual choices and behaviour, with the standard assumption being that people are rational and selfish (the so-called homo economicus). This microeconomic approach has, since the 1970s, also become dominant in macroeconomics, where macro theories are expected to be based on 'microfoundations'. PKE, in contrast, rejects methodological individualism and takes a holistic and historic approach. It is based on sociology and history rather than on the individual psychology of preferences or 'utility'.

There are two main reasons why PKE rejects standard microfoundations. First, PKE highlights the concept of fundamental uncertainty, as contrasted to risk. Risk refers to situations where the precise outcome is unknown, but the probability distribution is known. For example, in the case of rolling a dice, whilst we do not know in advance what number will be thrown, we *do* know that each number has a one-sixth chance of being thrown. Fundamental uncertainty, in contrast, refers to situations where even such probability distributions cannot be identified.

To illustrate, think of an entrepreneur contemplating investment in a steel factory in 1936. The expected returns from that factory will depend on the demand for steel in the coming years, which will depend, among other things, on whether there will be a war, how long it will last and how economic performance will be after the war – not to mention whether the factory itself will be destroyed by the war. A rational entrepreneur would have to give expected values and probability distributions for all of these scenarios – in a situation where World War II had not even begun! The example may be extreme, but PKE contends that investment decisions are usually made under conditions of fundamental uncertainty. Fundamental uncertainty is not a statement about the limited cognitive ability of humans to make forecasts but a statement about the nature of social reality. Societies do not work like a clock, where a future state can be readily deduced from a present state, but rather involve human agency, emergent properties and irreversibilities. The same is also true, therefore, of the economy.

So how do people make decisions in such an uncertain world? First, Keynes, in a famous phrase, uses the term 'animal spirits' to describe an innate drive to action rather than inaction. In other words, he argues that there are non-rational, creative impulses that are key to human behaviour. Second, he highlights the importance of social conventions. People will look at what other people are doing and evaluate their behaviour in light of these. Fundamental uncertainty is important for PK monetary theory because, as we will see below, it gives rise to 'liquidity preference' and is also key for understanding why investment expenditures tend to be highly unstable or, as Keynes says, appear to be driven by 'animal spirits' rather than rational calculation.

The second PK objection to the individualist approach is that economics needs 'macrofoundations' at least as much as 'microfoundations'. Societies are structured into social groups, including classes, which are of particular importance to the economy. Classes are social groups based on different functions within the economic process. The most famous ones are workers and capitalists, but the analysis can be extended to include rentiers and shareholders or to give a class analysis of gender relations. Members of a class have similar interests, usually similar incomes and typically form their own political and economic organisations to represent their interests. In capitalism, workers typically do not control the factories and own little, if any, wealth. They have to find a job in a world where involuntary unemployment is the norm, which puts them in a weak position relative to capitalists. Shareholders own firms or, more technically, the capital stock, and managers control the production process and make the investment decisions that play a key role in Keynesian macroeconomics.

The conflict between capital and labour is a permanent feature of capitalist society, and societies develop institutions to mediate and regulate the resulting class struggle. They also build welfare states and other social safety nets to cushion the extremes of unequal income distribution, as part of social compromise. In the PK view, social institutions are not mere distortions of a market process, but they play a constructive role in mediating social conflict.

The principle of effective demand

At the core of PK macroeconomics is the principle of effective demand: the idea that most of the time our economies are demand-constrained (as opposed to supply-constrained) so that the level of aggregate expenditures (on consumption, investment, government spending and net exports) determines the level of output in an economy. Economic fluctuations, i.e. the business cycle, are driven by changes in expenditures, and in particular investment expenditures. This is in sharp contrast to the neoclassical approach, where the idea of optimising agents always ensures that the economy is operating at full capacity, such that supply constraints control how much the economy produces (that's where the phrase 'supply-side' comes from).

In both PKE and neoclassical theory, the goods market will be in equilibrium if investment equals saving: only at this point will income equal expenditures and the economy can stably reproduce itself (ignoring for a moment state intervention and international trade). According to neoclassical economics, the level of saving in the economy determines the level of investment, so that levels of investment are controlled by how much people and businesses decide to save. For PKE, the causality goes the other way around, from investment to savings. Investment creates new income via the multiplier process, which in turn leads to additional saving. In this sense, investment is never constrained by *saving*, but it can be constrained by the *availability of finance and credit*, as discussed below.

Investment is the most volatile component of gross domestic product (GDP), and it is driven to a significant extent by animal spirits, i.e. by factors that cannot be reduced to rational behaviour. Investment expenditures depend on the expected return on the investments. The critical word here is 'expected'. The relevant rate of return is not a technologically given 'marginal product of capital' (i.e. the additional quantity of goods produced by adding an extra dollar's worth of capital to the production process) but is, rather, dependent on earnings expectations in the real world. This is where fundamental uncertainty becomes important. The formation of expectations is not strictly a rational process but a socio-psychological process that is prone to herd behaviour and overreaction.

People tend to save a bigger portion of their income as they get richer. This phenomenon is important for PKE, because when people save more, less of the money gets put directly into the economy as consumption. That means that income gains for poorer people have a higher economic 'multiplier' effect than they do for richer people, as some of the savings of richer people can sit idle and 'leak' out of circulation in the economy.

Typically, when people receive additional money they will spend some of it and save some of it – as opposed to spending or saving it all. Keynes called this a 'fundamental psychological law', and it is important because it means the multiplier for a national economy will (almost) always be greater than 1 (meaning each extra dollar spent will create more than 1 additional dollar of effective demand). Therefore, in the PKE theory an increase in investment expenditures will cause an increase in people's incomes and thus saving, as part of the new income is saved. Consumption expenditure, then, plays a passive role in Keynesian theory, and investment the active role, with national income as the adjusting variable.

In practice, multipliers also depend on import propensities and on tax rates. Modern PKE typically has multipliers that allow for different consumption propensities out of wage income and out of profit income because capitalists tend to be richer than workers. The multiplier then depends on income distribution. In applied research, the openness of an economy also has an important impact on the multiplier as trade openness represents a 'leakage' in the multiplier process, as some of the new income leaves the national economic system.

The goods market equilibrium is thus at the centre of Keynesian analysis. Notice, however, that this is a more limited notion of equilibrium than in neoclassical theory. This equilibrium is defined by incomes equalling expenditures, but unlike in neoclassical economics, there is no claim that a market equilibrium is socially optimal. Instead, within the PKE conception, equilibrium in the goods market usually comes with involuntary unemployment.

Unemployment and the futility of wage cuts

The labour market is, in the PK analysis, a subordinate market. Firms' hiring decisions will be determined most by their expected sales, with the cost of wages typically playing a secondary role. The equilibrium level of output set on the goods market will thus also determine the level of employment.

This is also true in the short run for many mainstream models, and in particular for the NAIRU (Non-Accelerating Inflation Rate of Unemployment) model, which theorizes that there is a hypothetical rate of unemployment at which inflation rates are stable. However, mainstream NAIRU models are anchored in an equilibrium rate of unemployment, which is determined purely by supply-side considerations in the long run. In other words, they re-introduce the 'classical' rules of the game in the long run.

PKE, on the other hand, emphasises that labour markets are social institutions that are adaptive even over longer time periods because of an endogenous labour supply or social wage norms. This results in what is called path dependence or hysteresis: labour markets have a 'memory', and increases in unemployment due to crisis can persist for a long time. In other words, PKE rejects the short-run/long-run dichotomy and argues that employment is governed by demand even over long time horizons. The NAIRU in PKE is thus not an anchored 'natural' rate, but is endogenous and changes with respect to demand shocks.

Debates about the long-run/short-run dichotomy aside, the difference between the Keynesian and the neoclassical analysis can best be understood when considering the effects of wage cuts in a recession. PKs argue that wage cuts will usually be counterproductive.

The key question that Keynes raises is whether a wage cut will necessarily lead to an increase in aggregate demand (in chapter 19 of the *General Theory*). His answer to this is 'no'. A wage cut will reduce the incomes of workers and, as a consequence, their consumption expenditure (which may also have a negative second-round effect on investment). A wage cut could induce firms to invest more, if firms are very sensitive to wage costs. However, that is unlikely in a recession because a recession means that firms already have difficulties selling what they have produced, so why should they produce more just because wages are falling?

It is more likely that firms will respond to the wage cut by reducing the prices they are charging, but then what we get is deflation rather than an increase in production. Deflation can have negative effects because it means that real debt burdens are increasing. With deflation, prices are falling, so the nominal income of firms will, for a given output level, also be falling. That is not necessarily a problem for firms in terms of financing their running costs, because wages and, presumably, other input costs will also be declining. But there is one key part of expenditures that is fixed in nominal terms: debt service. During deflation, the value of debt and of interest payments on debt increases relative to current income. Thus the more heavily indebted firms and households are, the more dangerous are the effects of deflation.[1]

Keynes discusses no fewer than eight channels by which a wage cut may affect demand (and thus employment) and identifies just one that can lead to positive effects during a recession: a wage cut will increase net exports if trade partners do not experience a similar wage cut. In practice the effectiveness of this channel will depend on how open the economy is to trade and what the economic condition is in other countries. It can work in a small open economy, when the rest of the world is growing healthily. Overall the verdict, however, is clear: a wage cut in a recession will normally not reduce unemployment. What is often euphemistically called 'labour market reform' will not work.

Modern PKE thus distinguishes between wage-led and profit-led demand regimes. In these models, an increase in wages will positively affect consumption but can have a negative impact on investment and (assuming that wage costs are stable in the trading partners) net exports. The relative size of these effects then determines whether the economy is overall wage-led or profit-led. In a wage-led demand regime, the consumption effect overpowers the investment and net export effect. This means an increase in wages will increase total demand and employment. In a profit-led regime the opposite is true – wage increases dampen investment and net exports enough to have a negative effect on demand and employment. There is an important distinction between the domestic effect and open economy effects. While individual countries can export themselves out of a crisis via exports, the world economy overall can't do that, because it is a closed economy (i.e. we can't rely on increased exports to Mars). Most PKE expect actual economies to be wage-led, at least domestically, and there is presently a lot of research to identify demand regimes empirically.

Monetary theory: endogenous money, liquidity preference and financial cycles

Keynesian theory of fundamental uncertainty has important implications not only for the theory of investment but also for monetary theory. While in mainstream/neoclassical economics, agents hold money essentially to buy goods and services (often called 'transactions demand' for money), in PKE money is held as a financial asset, rather than invested for potential returns. This may at first sound counterintuitive: why would anyone hold money which gives no yield? The answer is that in a world with uncertainty, what money offers is liquidity, i.e. flexibility. Holding money means earning no (or very little) interest, but it ensures the ability to buy assets in the next period. Other financial assets will offer higher returns, but they come with a risk of capital losses (or positively put: capital gains) and with the risk of the asset becoming illiquid. In normal times, this will mean that people will want to minimise their cash holding, because markets are liquid and reasonably predictable. However, in times of financial distress the demand for money, what Keynes called the 'liquidity preference', will go up sharply. Investors will hold money as an insurance against an uncertain future. In a financial crisis there will be a rush to liquidity – there will be a run on banks. This is also known as a liquidity trap: a situation when the public wants to hold money, independent of the interest rate. As a consequence other financial markets tend to freeze, such as happened in 2008 when interbank lending and commercial short-term lending and various other markets ceased functioning.

But where does the money come from in the first place? Money in a modern economy is essentially bank deposits. In other words, money is the short-term liabilities of the banking sector. It's an asset for everyone else (the non-financial sector) but a liability for the banks. The banking sector creates money as a side effect of its lending decisions. Typically, when banks extend credit, somewhere in the system deposits, i.e. money, will be created. This notion of money also implies that if loans are re-paid, money is destroyed. The lending decisions of banks will depend on their assessment of the creditworthiness of the applicants, which in turn will depend on their expected income streams and the market valuation of their collateral.

Central banks in this view do not control the money supply, as is taught in most textbooks, but rather set the base interest rate. They lend to banks and thereby create an anchor for the hierarchy of interest rates that the banks charge. The surcharge (above the central bank's base rate) that banks will charge for interest on loans will depend on the riskiness of loans and perceived uncertainty. Central banks can also use their balance sheets to buy financial assets, as has happened as part of Quantitative Easing, but this does not necessarily translate into an increase in circulating money (as measured e.g. by M2) if banks do not increase their lending. The PK view of endogenous money contrasts sharply with the Monetarist theory of an exogenous money supply under the control of the central bank. Monetarists believe that the central bank can control so-called base money and that the money multiplier (the relationship between base money and deposits) is stable. This model is still widely used in macroeconomics textbooks, but it is increasingly out of line with how central banks themselves conceive of the process of money creation.

The theory of endogenous money highlights the flexibility of the financial system. If a creditworthy firm has a reasonable investment project, the financial sector can, and in normal times will, provide the finance for investment. It is in this sense that investment is never constrained by savings but can be constrained by finance. If banks are worried about their balance sheet or don't share the expectations of the firm, credit may be restricted and firms' investment may indeed be constrained. The flexibility of the financial sector, however, is a double-edged sword as it will often lead to pro-cyclical movements in credit that amplify the business cycle, when banks share the same broad economic outlook as firms, i.e. when the animal spirits of firms and banks are aligned. In practice, the market value of collateral plays a key role in the assessment of creditworthiness. This also means that financial bubbles can easily inflate, as credit growth and asset prices (or real estate prices) form a positive feedback loop. Higher property prices lead to more collateral and higher lending; rapid credit growth fuels the property prices bubble. Hyman Minsky was one of the leading thinkers to develop Keynes' financial analysis into a theory of debt cycles and financial instability.

Economic policy

In the PK vision, capitalist market economies are prone to large fluctuations. Situations of full employment, while possible, will only occur by chance. PKE thus advocates extensive government involvement, but PKE is not associated with a particular political philosophy. While Keynes was a liberal, Kalecki was a socialist, who returned from the West to work in communist Poland in the 1950s. What PKs share is the sentiment that investment decisions should not be left to the market. Keynes famously, but opaquely, referred to this as 'the socialisation of investment'. The more liberally inclined would aim to achieve this by monetary and fiscal policy, but it may also be attempted by industrial policy, credit allocation or via state-owned enterprises. In the following we outline policy proposals that follow from PK analysis and contrast them to the current mainstream view on economic policy. This is for illustration, but it should be kept in mind that PKE is a set of theories about the working of capitalist economies, not a political ideology.

As mentioned above, in PKE market economies will not, in general, lead to full employment. Employment is determined by effective demand, which may fluctuate depending on changes in animal spirits and financial crises. This is the basic PK argument for extensive government intervention. Governments should use fiscal and monetary policy to increase demand and approximate full employment. Fiscal policy plays the key role in this approach because in times of crises, in particular after financial and debt over-hang crises, monetary policy will be limited in its effectiveness.

From this follows a view of government budget deficits that differs sharply from the mainstream. In an economic crisis, firms reduce their investment sharply and households will try to increase savings. As a result the private sector will want to save more and invest less – it moves to a net lending position. There are two ways this can be resolved: (1) either national income collapses such that private savings can equal investment, with mass unemployment resulting; or (2) some other sector has to move into a net borrowing position (and thereby stabilise national income). This is why government budget deficits in a crisis are a desirable outcome: they substitute the lacking private expenditures and thereby prevent unemployment. How long should the government run deficits? The short PK answer is: as long as there is substantial unemployment.

PKE regards financial markets as a potential source of instability because endogenous money creation can lead to boom–bust cycles and sustain asset price bubbles. Central banks thus have to use countercyclical monetary policy. The main instrument for this would be increased macroprudential regulation rather than interest rate policy. Most PKs are also sceptical about the benefits of international capital flows. International capital flows often reinforce financial bubbles (e.g. the Irish and Spanish real estate bubbles were importantly fuelled by capital inflows). Thus capital management or capital controls are part of the PK repertoire. Control of domestic monetary conditions is a precondition for effective national policies.

From the PK view there is no reason why monetary policy should be primarily con-cerned with inflation. Rather, central banks should be concerned with financial stability and with the overall level of economic activity, in particular the level of unemployment. So how would PK tackle inflation? For PKs (leaving aside the issue of inflation caused by price changes of imported goods like oil) the source of inflation is, most of the time, unresolved distributional conflicts. Thus the government should try to support social settlements that entail distributional compromises between capital and labour. Wage-bargaining institutions thus become useful social institutions, where social compromises can be forged, rather than a mere 'market imperfection'.

PK theory also has important implications for international economic relations, partic-ularly for international monetary arrangements like the Euro area. In these arrangements, when there are countries running trade surpluses and countries running trade deficits, the burden of adjustment falls entirely on the deficit countries. Such a system, which is actively enforced by the European Commission and the infamous Troika, results in a deflationary bias – i.e. those countries with current account deficits will have to reduce demand and/or suppress wages in order to gain competitiveness. If, on the other hand, those countries with current account surpluses (in the European case, Germany) were to adjust instead, they would have to stimulate domestic demand and foster wage growth to reduce their trade surpluses. Keynesian international arrangements would be such as to foster a balanced adjustment where surplus countries carry a substantial part of the burden of adjustment.

Note

1 The issue of deflation receives a somewhat schizophrenic treatment in modern main-stream economics. Standard macro textbooks typically assume an exogenous money supply. Deflation, i.e. a fall in prices, will then increase the real money supply and have an expansionary effect. Most modern central banks, however, are quite concerned about the danger of deflation and think that it has negative demand effects.

References

Arestis, P., McCauley, C. and Sawyer, M. (2001), 'An Alternative Stability Pact for the European Union', *Cambridge Journal of Economics*, Vol. 25, pp. 113–130.

Bhaduri, A. and Marglin, S. (1990), 'Unemployment and the Real Wage: The Economic Basis for Contesting Political Ideologies', *Cambridge Journal of Economics*, Vol. 14, No. 4, pp. 375–393.

Davidson, P. (1994), *Post Keynesian Macroeconomic Theory: A Foundation for Successful Economic Policies for the Twenty-First Century*, Aldershot: Edward Elgar.

Harcourt, G. (1969), 'Some Cambridge Controversies in the Theory of Capital', *Journal of Economic Literature*, Vol. 7, No. 2, pp. 369–405.

Hicks, J. (1937), 'Mr Keynes and the Classics: A Suggested Interpretation', *Econometrica*, Vol. 5, pp. 147–159.

Kaldor, N. (1956), 'Alternative Theories of Distribution', *Review of Economic Studies*, Vol. 23, No. 2, pp. 83–100.

Kalecki, M. (1965 [1954]), *Theory of Economic Dynamics*, New York: Monthly Review Press.

Keynes, J. (1937), 'The General Theory of Employment', *Quarterly Journal of Economics*, Vol. 41, No. 2, pp. 209–223.

Keynes, J. (1973[1936]), *The General Theory of Employment, Interest and Money*, The collected writings of John Maynard Keynes volume VII, Cambridge: Palgrave Macmillan.

King, J. (2002), *A History of Post Keynesian Economics Since 1936*, Cheltenham: Edward Elgar.

King, J. (2003), *The Elgar Companion to Post Keynesian Economics*, Cheltenham: Edward Elgar.

Lavoie, M. (2009), *Introduction to Post Keynesian Economics*, New York: Palgrave Macmillan.

Lavoie, M. (2014), *Post Keynesian Economics: New Foundations*, Aldershot: Edward Elgar.

Minsky, H. (1986), *Stabilizing an Unstable Economy*, New Haven: Yale University Press.

Moss, S. (1980), 'The End of Orthodox Capital Theory', in: Nell, E. (ed.), *Growth, Profits and Property: Essays in the Revival of Political Economy*, Cambridge: Cambridge University Press, pp. 64–79.

Palley, T. (1996), *Post Keynesian Economics: Debt, Distribution and the Macro Economy*, London: Palgrave Macmillan.

Robinson, J. (1956), *The Accumulation of Capital*, London: Palgrave Macmillan.

Sawyer, M. (1985), *The Economics of Michael Kalecki*, Basingstoke: Palgrave Macmillan.

Stockhammer, E. (2011), 'Wage Norms, Capital Accumulation and Unemployment: A Post Keynesian View', *Oxford Review of Economic Policy*, Vol. 27, No. 2, pp. 295–311.

Stockhammer, E., Onaran, Ö. and Ederer, S. (2009), 'Functional Income Distribution and Aggregate Demand in the Euro Area', *Cambridge Journal of Economics*, Vol. 33, No. 1, pp. 139–159.

Note on further readings

Classical PK writings include Keynes (1936), Kalecki (1965), Robinson (1956), Minsky (1986). King (2002) offers a good history of PKE. Lavoie (2009, 2014) are book-length introductions to PKE. A detailed structured bibliography on PKE can be found at www.postkeynesian.net/downloads/PKSG_Reading_list_2016. pdf. The most important journals for PKE are the *Cambridge Journal of Economics*, the *Journal of Post Keynesian Economics*, the *Review of Keynesian Economics*, and the *European Journal of Economics and Economic Policies*.

Marxist economics

Ben Fine and Alfredo Saad-Filho

Introduction

This chapter explains the essential elements of Marxist economics or, preferably, Marxist political economy (MPE). They include Marx's explanation of how and why wage workers are exploited, the systematic form taken by technical change through the growing use of machinery, the determinants of wages, prices and distribution, the role of the financial system and the recurrence of economic crises. This analysis provides the foundation for Marx's systemic critique of capitalism and his conclusion that the contradictions and limitations of this exploitative mode of production could be overcome only through the transition to a new mode, communism, through revolution if necessary. (In what follows, the terms communism and socialism are used as synonymous. For Marx, strictly speaking, socialism is the first or transition stage to communism, the latter taking an indeterminate time to be constructed.)

If such approaches, concepts and conclusions appear alien, it is because they have been marginalised in most academic institutions and in the media, to the extent that most economics departments completely bypass MPE and its potential contribution to a critical understanding of contemporary society. In the current age of neoliberalism, mainstream (orthodox or neoclassical) economics has tightened its grip on the discipline, dismissing heterodoxy in general and MPE in particular as failing the tests of logical, mathematical and/or statistical rigour. Yet, the shortcomings of the mainstream and the economic, environmental and geopolitical catastrophes spawned by capitalism have nurtured the search for alternatives among students of economics and, even more so, in other social sciences that address economic analysis more tolerantly than economics itself. In a world precariously balanced and afflicted by recurrent as well as persistent crises, the case for communism is open to be made, and it can rest upon a Marxist analysis both for its critique of capitalism and for the light it sheds on the potential for alternatives. Such a view stands in sharp contrast to the mainstream, for which commitment to the market is

entirely to the fore without questioning whether the market system, and the class relations it represents, remains appropriate.

This is also a timely moment for the historical renewal of interest in MPE as it has
always been validated as well as inspired by downturns in the capitalist economy. Nonetheless, it should also be acknowledged that Marx admired the dynamism of capitalism
in developing both levels of production and productivity, what he called the productive
forces, not least as he saw such developments as providing the potential for socialist alternatives both within capitalism itself (think of the welfare state and nationalised industries)
and through radical break with it. He was also acutely aware that capitalism's extraordinary capacity to develop the productive forces is both constrained and misdirected by
its commitment to private profit as opposed to collective forms of ownership, control,
distribution and consumption. The consequences are evident in the dysfunctions and
inequities of contemporary life.

The method and approach of MPE

At the time of this writing, with the Global Financial Crisis (GFC) ongoing since 2007,
many students have realised the limitations of what they are being taught as economics
and are actively campaigning for pluralism in their curriculum and for the teaching of
alternative approaches, MPE amongst them. On the other hand, what they are being and
have been taught as neoclassical economics has not only gone to the opposite extreme in
terms of its own extraordinary narrowness but has exhibited limited willingness, let alone
capacity, to allow for alternatives. This is despite the loss of intellectual legitimacy that
has accompanied the GFC: not only did the mainstream not see it coming, but it cannot
explain or remedy the crisis after the event.

Student grievances with neoclassical economics range over a number of its features.
First and foremost, neoclassical economics depends upon mathematical models and a
corresponding deductive method at the almost exclusive expense of other forms of rea-
soning. By the same token, this method is both ahistorical and asocial, most obviously
in depending upon production and utility functions that bear little or no relationship to
the society to which they are applied. Slaves and slave owners, serfs and lords, men and
women (across all societies and times), as well as capitalists and workers, are indiscrimi-
nately presumed to be motivated in exactly the same way, to maximise their self-interest,
whether expressed as profit, 'utility' or whatever. By contrast, whilst economic motives
play an enormous role in MPE, how they are formed and pursued in different social
and historical circumstances (slavery is not capitalism; the home is not the marketplace)
is of paramount importance. Indeed, for MPE, it is imperative that the concepts used
and developed correspond to their object of study, as will be shown below for the cen-
trepiece of MPE, the labour theory of value (LTV).

The arbitrary and perverse assumptions that follow from its dependence upon *'homo
economicus'*, rationality, given preferences and single motivation of self-interest, are other

aspects of dissatisfaction with the mainstream. This is not just because these starting points defy our experience, but they also preclude many vital questions, such as why do we have the preferences we have and why do we behave in the ways that we do. Paradoxically, the mainstream's much-vaunted celebration of the freedom of choice of the individual in market society is nothing of the sort. Within that theory, what the individual chooses is entirely pre-determined by given preferences (or utility function) without space for either inventiveness or identity on the part of the individual subject, thereby allowing supply and demand to be mathematically and rigidly derived.

In contrast, MPE, like much other social science other than mainstream economics, asks how such individual subjectivity is conditioned by social structures. MPE takes social classes, rather than individuals, as its starting point for understanding the nature of the economy both historically and socially. As already suggested by reference to slavery and capitalism, and so on, there are clear differences between forms of economic organisation. In particular, class society is about who works, how, and for whom, with what consequences and, not least, who gets to exploit whom in the sense of appropriating surplus production without having worked for it except through ownership or exaggerated rewards for exercising control and management. Just as under a monarchy, not everyone can be the king or queen, so not everyone can choose to be a capitalist under capitalism; otherwise, there would be no workers. For capitalism, then, MPE starts with the broad and fundamental distinction between those who are wage workers and those who employ them. It has long been recognised, not uniquely by MPE, that capitalism is based on exploitation in the sense that workers do not receive in wages all that they produce. Even setting aside the resources needed for the renewal of production and gross investment, 'rewards' also accrue to property owners in the form of profit, interest and rent as well as bloated 'salaries' for the functionaries of capitalist production and exchange and social control. As will be seen below, the uniqueness of MPE lies in how it conceptualises and explains such exploitation and draws out its consequences for understanding the nature, dynamics, contradictions and limitations of capitalism.

The contrast with neoclassical economics could not be greater. While the latter perceives the economy as a collection of individuals more or less efficiently organised through the market, MPE is systemic (holistic), identifying economy-wide structures, processes, agents and relations and classes as opposed to individuals simply related through market supply and demand. Then, on this basis, forces for change are identified that drive the economy and create tensions in doing so that can at most be temporarily resolved; that is, the capitalist economy is driven to grow but can only do so by creating the possibility of crises.

In this respect, there are two further contrasts between MPE and the mainstream. First is that it is inappropriate to understand the capitalist (or any other) economy in terms of 'equilibrium', since it is never achieved in practice, and its analytical use obscures the sources of conflicts and dynamics within the economy. Second is that the forces for change have to be identified and analysis taken further in understanding their implications and how they interact with one another. Within MPE, this is a source of continuing controversy ranging over whether, for example, the leading drivers of the economy are wages or profits, how parasitic a role is played by finance, and what is happening to the determinants of profitability.

The labour theory of value

At the heart of debates within MPE and between MPE and other schools of thought in economics is the nature and validity of Marx's labour theory of value (LTV). For many, the LTV is to be understood as a theory of price – for example, do commodities exchange at prices that can be derived algebraically from the labour time required to produce them? Note, first, that such labour time does not just involve what is called the 'living' labour or the time of those working on the current product, but also the ('dead', 'embodied' or 'congealed') labour that has gone previously into producing the raw materials and equipment required in production.

Many political economists have been attracted by the LTV, not least Adam Smith and David Ricardo, but each has found it unsatisfactory. One reason given is that it takes no account of the different capital intensities of production, that is, commodities produced with a higher quantity of capital (e.g., capital-intensive nuclear energy in contrast with the more labour-intensive construction industry) or which take longer to produce (aeroplanes in contrast with restaurant meals). In either case, commodities should have a price including a premium corresponding to the amount of capital advanced and the time for which it is advanced and on which a larger profit will be expected in order to equalise the rate of profit of the advanced capitals. Given these logical imperatives, both Smith and Ricardo realised that prices will systematically diverge from the labour time taken to produce them. At a further remove, (changes in) demand will affect prices, however temporarily, as will rents and monopolies.

For reasons such as these, the LTV has been subject to longstanding rejection, even from those sympathetic to other aspects of MPE, especially its emphasis on class and exploitation. Significantly, Marx was well aware of these problems and did take them into account. How and whether satisfactorily remains a key element of debate if not covered here in detail.

There is, though, good reason for such debate, because what fundamentally divides interpretations of Marx are two different ways of understanding the LTV, and these are irreconcilable. One proceeds as laid out above. How well can (labour) value explain price quantitatively – not very well, so either modify or reject it. The other, and reflecting Marx's own approach, begins from a very different sort of question. Under what circumstances does value as measured by labour time exist within society rather than simply in the minds of would-be economists as a good or bad explanation of the level of prices? Marx's answer is deceptively simple: only in a (basically capitalist) society where commodity production is pervasive do different types of labour become measured against one another by society itself through the exchange mechanism. Whatever labour has been contributed to the production of commodities either in the past or in the present is thrown into the great melting pot of exchange. And all the different types of labour are rendered as equivalent to, or more exactly measurable against, one another in terms of the prices they command.

Of course, this does not mean that all labours count the same. The more skilled will count as more labour than the less skilled, and labours of the same skill and even similar tasks may count differently once account is taken of any number of considerations, such as the capital-intensity of production (see above), presence of monopoly, payment of rent, etc. But the prior issue for Marx is to recognise that capitalist commodity production is a system that connects production by wage labour with the buying and selling of commodities for profit, and he sets himself, and us, the task of tracing the journeys taken by the products of that labour in production to their distant destinations in exchange.

As stated earlier, this is far from being a theory of equilibrium prices – the basis on which Marx's value theory tends to be rejected. More specifically, Marx's first concern is with how a system based on free market exchange can generate profits while, simultaneously, concealing the capture of surplus labour from the wage workers. In contrast, under slavery or feudalism the exploitation of the direct producers is obvious. Marx's second concern is with how profits can increase, especially through the development of new methods and processes of production under capitalism (from simple manufacture to the factory system, for example, something that tends to be overlooked by casual use of the ubiquitous production function). Furthermore, what it is like to be a worker under capitalism both individually and collectively, in the workplace as well as beyond it in society more generally (for example, what are the implications for the family, civil society and the state, that the economy is capitalistic?). Marx's third concern is with the economic and social consequences of how capitalist production evolves (increasingly under corporate or, today, financial control, for example), and how such developments prepare the ground for moving beyond capitalism.

Commodities, labour and value

To meet these concerns, Marx begins his analysis on the basis that commodities exchange at their values (their labour time of production). This allows him to uncover exploitation under capitalism without entering into complex considerations of price formation. His explanation rests upon specifying the class relations of capitalism, notably between capital and labour. Whilst, as a class, capitalists own the means of production, the class of labour can only gain access to work and a reasonable livelihood by selling their ability to work as wage-labourers. For Marx, the distinction between the ability to work and the work itself is decisive in understanding capitalism, and it is the capacity to work, which he called labour-power, that is bought and sold, not labour itself (which is the activity of work rather than something that can be bought and sold like cheese). With the wage being paid for labour-power, how much labour is actually performed and with what quality is a matter of conflict between capital and labour (although there are other conflicts too, such as over levels of wages and working conditions). By analogy, you can hire a car (like you hire a worker), but that is quite different from how far, fast and safely you drive it (or him/her).

Consider, then, Marx's reconstruction of the LTV, starting with commodities. These are goods and services produced for sale, rather than consumption by their own producers. Commodities have two common features. First, they are use values: they have some useful characteristic. The nature of their use, whether it derives from physiological need, social convention, fancy or vice is irrelevant in the first instance as far as their value is concerned. Second, commodities have exchange value (they can command a price on a market): they can, in principle, be exchanged for other commodities in specific ratios. Exchange value or price shows that, despite their distinct use values, commodities are equivalent (at least in one respect) to one another in terms of commanding a monetary equivalent.

The double nature of commodities, as use values with exchange value, has implications for labour. On the one hand, commodity-producing labour is what is termed concrete labour, that is labour producing specific use values such as clothes, food or books (performed, respectively, by tailors, farmers and publishers). On the other hand, when goods are produced for exchange, they have a relationship of equivalence to one another. In this case, labour is also 'abstract' or general in some sense (the amount of labour is what counts, not what type it is). Just like commodities themselves, commodity-producing labour is both general and specific. Concrete labours exist in all societies because people always need to produce a variety of use values for their own survival. In contrast, abstract labour as just described is historically specific; it exists only where commodities are being produced *and* exchanged.

Abstract labour has two distinct aspects – qualitative and quantitative – that should be analysed separately. First, abstract labour derives from the relationship of equivalence between commodities. Even though it is historically contingent, abstract labour has real existence; it is not merely a construct of the economist's mind, as is shown by the possibility in principle of actually exchanging the product of one's labour for the product of anyone else's labour (through money). The ability of money to purchase any commodity shows that money represents the presence of this abstract labour.

Second, the reality of exchange values shows that there is a quantitative relationship between the abstract labours necessary to produce each type of different commodity. However, this relationship is not directly visible in the sense that, when we purchase something, the different types of labour that have gone into making it, and how they were performed, and how much they count, are not apparent in the price. However hard we look at a commodity, we cannot see how it has been produced, physically to a large extent, and how much and many concrete labours have gone into it, let alone the social relations between capital and labour in the production process. This is so for market participants themselves as well as for those scholars of the economy purely concerned with supply and demand.

For example, in his *Inquiry into the Nature and Causes of the Wealth of Nations*, first published in 1776, Adam Smith claimed that in 'early and rude' societies goods exchanged directly in proportion to the labour time necessary to produce them. For example, if it usually costs twice the labour to kill a beaver as to kill a deer, one beaver should 'naturally' exchange for two deer. However, Smith believes that this simple pricing rule breaks down when instruments and machines are used in production. The reason is that, in addition to the workers, the owners of 'stock' (capital) also have a claim to the value of the product in the form of profit (and landowners to a rent). Since these claims must be added to the price, the LTV becomes invalid.

Marx disagrees with Smith, for two reasons. First, 'simple' or 'direct' exchange (in proportion to labour time of production) is not typical of any human society; this is simply a construct of Smith's mind – in his rude society, you would just go and catch whatever you wanted rather than specialise for exchange, which requires a commodity-producing society. Second, and more importantly for our purposes, although commodity exchanges are based on the quantitative relations of equivalence between different types of labour, this relationship is indirect. In other words, whereas Smith abandons his own 'labour theory of value' at the first hurdle (the obscuring presence of profits and rents to the dependence of value on labour time), Marx develops his own value analysis rigorously and systematically into a cogent explanation of the values that underpin commodity prices under capitalism.

Indeed, Marx called 'commodity fetishism' the limitation of the understanding of commodities to the surface (self-evident) relations between price and use (or utility) as opposed to labour and other invisible relations by which commodities come to the market. For Marx, the significance of his theory of commodity fetishism lay in how it went beyond treating exchange relations as relations between things (the prices at which goods exchange with one another) to unravel the social relations between those who produce those things. In short, piercing through commodity fetishism allows for the exploitative relations attached to capitalism to be revealed.

Capital and capitalism

Commodities have been produced for thousands of years. However, in non-capitalist societies commodity production is generally marginal, and most goods and services are produced for direct consumption rather than for market exchange. It is different in capitalist societies. *A first distinguishing feature of capitalism is the generalised production of commodities.* Under capitalism, the market is foremost, most workers are employed in the production of commodities, and firms and households regularly purchase commodities as production inputs and final goods and services, respectively.

A second distinguishing feature of capitalism is the production of commodities for profit. In capitalist society, commodity owners typically do not merely seek to make a living – they want to (and must) make profit (to survive). Therefore, the production decisions and the level and structure of employment, and the living standards of the society, are grounded in the profitability of enterprise.

A third distinguishing feature of capitalism is wage labour. Like commodity production and money, wage labour first appeared thousands of years ago. However, before capitalism wage labour was always limited, and other forms of labour were predominant. For example, co-operation within small social groups, slavery in the great empires of antiquity, serfdom under feudalism, and independent production for subsistence or exchange have prevailed across all types of society. Wage labour has become the typical mode of labour only recently – three or four hundred years ago in England, and often much later elsewhere.

Neoclassical economic theory defines capital as an ensemble of things, including means of production, money and financial assets. More recently, knowledge and community relations have been designated as human or social capital. For Marx, this is nonsensical. Those objects, assets and human attributes have always existed, whereas capitalism is historically new. It is misleading to extend the concept of capital where it does not belong, as if it were valid universally or throughout history. A horse, hammer or one million dollars may or may not be capital; that depends on the context in which they are used. If they are engaged in production for profit through the direct or indirect employment of wage labour, then they are capital; otherwise, they are simply animals, tools or banknotes.

For MPE, capital involves class relation, but these relations are often reduced to their (immediately apparent) physical attributes or, as Marx puts it, as relations between things rather than people. Moreover, capital is not merely a general relationship between the producers and sellers of commodities, or a market relationship of supply and demand. Instead, it involves *class relations of exploitation.* This social relationship includes two classes, defined by their ownership, control and use of the means of production (MP), or inputs, whether human or physical. On the one hand are the capitalists, who own the MP, employ workers and own what they produce; on the other hand are the wage workers, who are employed by the capitalist and engage directly in production without any ownership rights over what they produce.

Most people do not freely choose to become wage workers. Historically, wage labour expands, and capitalist development takes off, only as the peasants, artisans and the self-employed lose control of the means of production, or as non-capitalist forms of production become unable to provide for subsistence. The much-repeated claim that the wage contract is the outcome of a free bargain between equals is, therefore, both partial and misleading. Even though the workers are free to apply for one job rather than another, they are almost always in a weak bargaining position when facing their (prospective) employers. The wage workers need money to attend to the pressing needs of their household. This is both the stick and the carrot with which capitalist society forces the workers to sign up 'freely' to the labour contract, 'spontaneously' turn up for work, and 'voluntarily' satisfy the expectations of their line managers.

From value to surplus value

The capitalists combine the inputs to production, generally purchased from other capitalists, with the labour of wage workers hired on the market to produce commodities for sale at a profit. The circuit of industrial capital captures the essential aspects of factory production, farm labour, office work and other forms of capitalist production. It can be represented as follows:

$$M - C <_{LP}^{MP} \ldots P \ldots C' - M'$$

The circuit starts when the capitalist advances money (M) to purchase two types of commodities (C), inputs (MP) and labour-power (LP). During production (. . . P . . .) the workers transform the inputs into new commodities (C') that are sold for more money (M').

Marx calls surplus value the difference between M' and M. Surplus value is the source of industrial and commercial profit and other forms of surplus revenue such as interest and rent. We now identify the source of surplus value, which Marx considered one of his most significant achievements.

Surplus value cannot arise purely out of exchange. Although some can profit from the sale of commodities above their value (unequal exchange), for example unscrupulous traders and speculators, this is not possible for every seller for two reasons. First, the sellers are also buyers. If every seller surcharged customers by 10 per cent, say, such gains would be lost to the suppliers, and no extra profit would arise from this exercise. Therefore, although some can become rich by robbing or outwitting others, this is not possible for society as a whole, and unequal exchanges cannot provide a general explanation for profit: 'cheating' only transfers value, it does not create new value. Second, competition tends to increase supply in any sector offering exceptional profits, eventually eliminating the advantages of individual luck or cunning. Therefore, surplus value (or profit in general) must be explained for society as a whole, or systemically, rather than relying on individual merit or expertise.

Now, inspection of the circuit of capital shows that surplus value is the difference between the value of the output, C', and the value of the inputs, MP and LP. Since this difference cannot be due to unequal exchange, the value increment must derive from somewhere in the process of production. More specifically, for Marx, it arises from the use in production of a commodity, which must have the property not only of being able to create new value but also more new value than it itself cost. Which input is this?

Starting from the means of production (physical inputs), Marx is very clear that, on their own, the transformation of the inputs into the output does not create new value. The presumption that the transformation of things into other things could produce value regardless of context or human intervention confuses the two aspects of the commodity, use value and exchange value. It implies that an apple tree, when it produces apples from soil, sunlight and water, creates not only the use value but also the value of the apples, and that ageing wine, for example, spontaneously adds value (rather than merely use value) to the wine without any further labour to do so. The naturalisation of value relations begs the question of why commodities have value, whereas many products of nature, goods and services, have no economic value: sunlight, air, access to public beaches and parks, favours exchanged between friends and so on.

Thus, value is not a product of nature (although dependent upon it) nor a substance physically embodied in the commodities: value is a social relation between commodity producers that appears as exchange value, a relationship between things. Goods and services possess value only under certain social and historical circumstances. The value relation develops fully only under capitalism, in tandem with the production of commodities, the use of money, the diffusion of wage labour, and the generalisation of market-related property rights.

With value understood as a social relation typical of commodity societies, its source – and the origin of surplus value – must be the performance of commodity-producing labour (the productive consumption of the commodity labour-power) rather than the using or making of things in general. As the inputs are physically blended into the output, their value is transferred, and it forms part of the value of the output. In addition to the transfer of the value of the inputs, labour simultaneously adds new value to the product. In other words, whereas the physical inputs contribute value because of the labour time necessary elsewhere and previously deployed to produce them as commodities, freshly performed labour contributes new value to the output.

The value of the output is equal to the value of the inputs plus the value added by the workers during production. Since the value of the means of production is merely transferred, *production is profitable only if the value added exceeds the wage costs*. That is, surplus value is the difference between the value added by the workers and the value of labour-power. Put another way, wage workers are exploited because they work for longer than the time it takes to produce the goods that they can purchase with their wages. For the rest of their working time, the workers are exploited – they produce (surplus) value for the capitalists.

Just as the workers have little choice on the matter of being exploited, the capitalists cannot avoid exploiting the workers. Exploitation through the extraction of surplus value is a systemic feature of capitalism: this system of production operates like a pump for the extraction of surplus value. The capitalists must exploit their workers if they are to remain in business; the workers must concur in order to satisfy their immediate needs; and exploitation is the fuel that moves capitalist production and exchange.

It is important to note that, although the wage workers are exploited, they need not be poor in absolute terms (relative poverty, due to the unequal distribution of income and wealth, is a completely different matter). The development of technology increases the productivity of labour, and it potentially allows even the poorest members of society to enjoy relatively comfortable lifestyles, however high the rate of exploitation might be.

Profit and (increasing) exploitation

Firm profits can increase in many different ways. For example, the capitalists can compel their workers to work longer hours or work harder (greater intensity of labour), employ better-skilled workers, or change the technology of production.

All else constant, longer working days produce more profit because more output is possible at little extra cost (the land, buildings, machines and management structures being the same). This is why capitalists always claim that the reduction of the working week hurts profits and, therefore, lowers output and employment. However, in reality, other things are not constant, and historical experience shows that such reductions can be neutral or even lead to higher productivity because of their effects on worker efficiency and morale. Outcomes vary depending on the circumstances, and they may be strongly negative for some capitalists and advantageous for others.

Greater labour intensity condenses more labour into the same working time. Increasing worker effort, speed and concentration raises the level of output and reduces unit costs; therefore, profitability rises. The employment of better trained and educated workers leads to similar outcomes. They can produce more commodities, and create more value, per hour of labour.

Marx calls the additional surplus value extracted through longer hours, more intense labour or extending work to women and children absolute surplus value. This type of surplus value involves the expenditure of more labour, whether in the same working day or in a longer day, with given wages and methods of production. Absolute surplus value was especially important in early capitalism, when the working day was often stretched as long as fourteen or sixteen hours. More recently, absolute surplus value has been extracted through the lengthening of the working week and the penetration of work into leisure time (work often extends into the weekend and holidays, and the availability of mobile phones and computers allows the employees to be always on call). Moreover, the workers are frequently compelled to increase productivity through more intense labour (e.g., faster production lines or reduced breaks) or coerced into acquiring new skills in their 'free' time (e.g., attending courses). Despite its importance, absolute surplus value is limited both physically and socially. It is impossible to increase the working day or the intensity of labour indefinitely, and the workers gradually come to resist these forms of exploitation, eventually winning at least some battles (although such gains are far from universal and remain under threat when achieved).

Rather than increasing the surplus merely by extending the work done, capitalists can raise profitability by increasing productivity, primarily through the introduction of new technology and new machines, thus reducing the labour that goes into contributing to the wage. How can this be done? First, the production process is divided up into tasks to which particular labourers are allocated. Second, tools are developed for these tasks. Third, mechanical power is used. Finally, these developments are brought together in machinery, itself housed within a factory system.

Marx terms this the production of relative surplus value. On this basis, he develops a sophisticated understanding of how production develops under capitalism (not least by contrast with the eponymous production function to be found in neoclassical economics). Like Adam Smith before him, Marx also highlights how such developments tend to strip workers of their traditional skills and reduce them to machine minders (although new skills are created in caring for and developing machinery), reinforcing the idea that how much work is done and with what productivity is of paramount importance. Marx, however, went far beyond Smith in exploring the consequences of such capitalist development of production. In particular, he recognised how competition between capitalist producers was fought largely on the basis of size of capital controlled, in order to lead in productivity through the largest and most powerful factories. This gave rise to Marx's famous phrase describing capitalist imperatives: 'Accumulate, accumulate, that is Moses and the prophets!'

For Marx, then, the major, systematic source of productivity increase involves working up more inputs into final products by a given amount of labour in a given time (although there can be other sources of technical change, not least the invention of new products, materials and processes). In sum, relative surplus value is more flexible than absolute surplus value, and it has become the most important form of exploitation under modern capitalism, because productivity growth can outstrip wage increases for long periods.

MPE, laws of development and contemporary capitalism

Marx is universally praised for his analysis of how production develops under capitalism. But he also derives economic *and* social consequences from his analysis of production and the accumulation of capital. For the economy, he shows how capitalism (a) develops unevenly as a world economy, with wealth and poverty as opposite sides of the same coin both within and between nations; (b) increases and concentrates corporate power; (c) depends upon a sophisticated financial system that can sustain growth but prompt deep crises; and (d) renders unemployment both inevitable and volatile. And, for the society in which the capitalist economy is embedded, Marx is acutely conscious of how the provision of health, education and welfare, let alone access to, and exercise of, political and ideological power, are subordinated to the imperatives of profitability. Progress, or not, in these areas is contingent on the ways and extent to which working people can press for and sustain reforms, only for these reforms to be vulnerable to the power of capitalists and their representatives, especially in the context of crisis, recession and 'austerity'.

These insights remain of relevance for our understanding of contemporary capitalism, suitably developed to include economic and social developments, not least those concerning the rise of neoliberalism, its attachment to financialisation and the uneven incidence of, and responses to, the GFC. Dealing with these issues is beyond the scope of this chapter, although, as with MPE more generally, it is important to recognise how closely debated are such issues. In these respects, the contrast with mainstream economics is also sharp. Whilst the latter has sought to spread its scope of analysis by applying its methods beyond the market (as in institutional economics, development economics, economic sociology or, indeed, the 'economics of everything'), it does so on the basis of its reduced and flawed analytical principles, if possibly supplemented by an added wrinkle or two, with behavioural economics to the fore, to complement, if inconsistently, utility maximisation. This is more a plundering of the social sciences than interdisciplinarity, for which MPE seeks to explain the social in light of the economic, not to reduce it to the falsely perceived economic.

Conclusion

In principle, MPE offers the strongest intellectual threat to the mainstream as well as supporting the most acute political challenge to capitalism. So it is unsurprising that MPE is shunned relentlessly in mainstream teaching and research. By contrast, neoclassical economics is extreme in all respects across reliance upon methodological individualism, mathematical methods, empirical methods, the positive–normative dualism, equilibrium and so on, whereas MPE challenges on all of these fronts, seeing other economic theories as partial reflections of reality (think of utility and production functions as exemplary illustrations of commodity fetishism!).

Despite these uncompromising critiques, MPE recognises that exploitation through the extraction of surplus value renders capitalism uniquely able to develop technology and the forces of production. This is the main reason why Marx admires the progressive features of capitalism. However, he *also* points out that capitalism is the most destructive mode of production in history. The profit motive is blind, and it can be overwhelming. It has led to astonishing discoveries and unsurpassed improvements in living standards, especially (but not exclusively) in the 'core' Western countries. In spite of this, capitalism has also led to widespread destruction and degradation of the environment and of human lives. Profit-seeking has led to slavery, genocide, brutal exploitation of workers and the uncontrolled destruction of the environment, with long-term global implications. Capitalism also generates and condones the mass unemployment of workers, machinery and land in spite of unsatisfied wants, and tolerates poverty even though the means to abolish it are readily available. Capitalism can extend human life, but it can empty it of rewarding meaning (as with the diseases of affluence). It supports unparalleled achievements in human education and culture while fostering greed, mendacity, sexual and racial discrimination and other forms of human oppression.

These contradictory effects of capitalism are inseparable. Private ownership of the means of production and market competition *necessarily* give rise to the wage relation, exploitation through the extraction of surplus value, and they facilitate crises, war and other negative features of capitalism. This places a strict limit on the possibility of social, political and economic reforms, and on the capacity of the market to assume a 'human face'. Limitations such as these led Marx to conclude that capitalism can be overthrown, and communism created, opening the possibility of realisation of the potential of the vast majority through the elimination of the irrationalities and human costs of capitalism.

Despite all this, MPE is not currently in a strong position to influence political developments, and this situation is unlikely to change through the 'implosion' of neoclassical economics because of its internal inconsistencies or external criticism. The continuity and renewal of MPE depends, instead, on developments outside academia, especially on the fortunes of the workers in class struggle, which could potentially bring to light once again the connections between theory and practice that are at the core of Marxism. Nonetheless, revival of MPE is vital to sustain alternatives to the mainstream as part and parcel of a broader commitment to rethinking economics and those seeking the framing of alternatives.

In this light, what policy alternatives might MPE offer, especially given what are generally presumed to be the failed twentieth-century attempts at constructing socialism? Marx was not unduly concerned to construct what he critically referred to as socialist utopias, preferring to envisage socialism as emerging out of working-class organisation and struggles against capitalism. This certainly seemed to be on the agenda during the post-war boom when trade unions and their political organisations exercised considerable power and future prospects seem to rest on whether social reformism (and decolonisation) might continue to allow for growth and prosperity, with socialist revolution as a potential alternative.

The end of the post-war period and the rise of neo-liberalism have taken the contest between social reformism and social revolution off the agenda. In addition, the leading source of power in economic and, increasingly, social organisation has been occupied by finance which, if anything, has even strengthened its hold in the wake of the GFC, despite its guilt by association with the crisis and its powerlessness to resolve the crisis' consequences. For many, then, looking back to the so-called Keynesian golden age, future prospects rest on putting finance back in its place, conveniently overlooking that Keynesianism experienced its own crisis.

MPE continues to debate intensively amongst itself about the extent to which finance is a cause as opposed to a symptom of the GFC and its aftermath. Where there might be agreement is that overcoming the power of finance is a necessary, but far from sufficient condition for strengthening the hand of working people in developing both alternative forms of organisation and policies themselves, ones that bring to the majority the power, control and well-being from which they are currently denied in deference to an increasingly narrow and more powerful elite.

Recommended readings

Callinicos, A. (2014), *Deciphering Capital: Marx's Capital and Its Destiny*, London: Bookmarks.

Fine, B. and Saad-Filho, A. (2013), *The Elgar Companion to Marxist Economics*, Aldershot: Edward Elgar.

Fine, B. and Saad-Filho, A. (2016), *Marx's Capital*, Sixth Edition, London: Pluto Press.

Harvey, D. (2010), *A Companion to Marx's Capital*, London: Verso.

Weeks, J. (2010), *Capital, Exploitation and Crises*, London: Routledge.

3 Austrian economics

Xavier Méra and Guido Hülsmann

The economics profession is said to be in a crisis, for it failed to announce the 2008 meltdown. The widespread perception is that the few economists who predicted it, with various degrees of precision, are usually followers of one 'heterodox' school of thought or another. Accordingly, 'orthodox' or 'mainstream' economics has especially been targeted for criticism, but what is orthodox in economics, today? How can we define the mainstream? Such expressions cannot refer to some unified grand theory that most economists agree on. There is no such theory. Whether we look at textbook microeconomics or at Keynesian-inspired macroeconomics, 'orthodoxy' is simply a rhetorical shorthand for several more or less independent theoretical developments, which today are taken to be the standard approaches to the issues they are designed to deal with.

Nevertheless, there is one view that all economists are supposed to hold, one view which may be considered as a defining feature of the mainstream: in order for an explanation to be truly scientific, it must be obtained and framed in a certain way. It must be modelled after the natural sciences, which explain observed facts by pointing out that these facts are always quantitatively related in a certain way to other observed facts (e.g., in a closed system, the speed of all particles is related to the temperature and the pressure prevailing in the system). And this general idea about what science is and does ('positivism') naturally leads to the idea that economic theories should be evaluated according to their predictive power. The widespread failure to predict the crisis then naturally leads to scepticism. After all, the mainstream failed according to its own standards.

Among the economists who anticipated the coming meltdown, one finds some Austrian economists. This is especially noteworthy because prediction of specific events does not have for Austrians the central role it has for mainstream economists. Austrians typically do not conceive of economics as some junior natural science. They do not believe that one can explain data with other data. In the distinctive methodology of 'a priorism' as put forward by Ludwig von Mises, it is held that the core of economics is made of propositions that cannot be falsified or verified by confronting theory to observed experience. In this view, economic laws of cause and effect are logically deduced from the very nature of human action.

This feature alone is sufficient for Austrian economics to be considered as a heterodox school and an 'unscientific' one according to the mainstream standards. In order to make the reader aware of what Austrian economics is and why it is scientific, according to its adherents, we will therefore first say a few things about its method, by contrasting it to the orthodox way of practicing economics. Then we will present Austrian-style analyses of the crisis and discuss why some Austrians were able to understand what was going on prior to 2008 and after.

The disagreement in economics over method: Austrians versus the mainstream

The prevailing method of causal analysis, in mainstream economics, consists of the following: first, one observes some phenomenon. For instance, unemployment has increased from one decade to the next. Then, one looks out for other observable phenomena which seem to be correlated with the first, say, spending in the economy has decreased or the legal minimum wage in the relevant area has been raised. Based on those intuitive correlations, one proposes some working hypothesis which could explain them, such as the Keynesian view that employment derives ultimately from the level of aggregate spending in the economy or the view that a minimum-wage law forces part of the workforce into unemployment when the minimum-wage rate is above some market clearing level. In order to find out how robust the hypothesised explanations are, one will then need to deduce from them still other predictions and observe how prescient they turn out to be. As data are gathered and tests are conducted to verify if the set of expected correlations hold between the phenomenon of unemployment and its hypothesised cause, as well as between the other related cause-and-effect relationships, the hypothesis becomes more or less confirmed or falsified. Depending on the outcome, more or less drastic modifications of the theory may be required, or the hypothesis may be discarded in favour of a new one to which the same process will be applied. As time goes on, ever more generalisations of non-falsified theories are proposed, and the body of scientific knowledge grows by filtering out the most dubious explanations.

Austrians criticise this method on two accounts, one which might be considered as a practical difficulty, whereas the other one is more fundamental.

The practical one is that in order to test the predicted relationship, one would need to hold constant every variable which could have some impact on the outcome except for the one which is under examination. Now that might not be a problem whenever the scientist is able to isolate the relevant relationships in laboratory experiments, but there is no laboratory available in which one can reproduce a complex society. In addition, any variable could conceivably have some influence on the outcome, and only some of the virtually innumerable variables one needs to hold constant are known to begin with.

More fundamentally, Austrians typically point out that, in order for various tests to be considered as confirmations or falsifications of the previous ones, one must *presuppose* that human beings deal with a situation in always the same way whenever it presents itself again. This raises three serious problems. The first one is that this presupposition cannot be observed and tested; therefore, any 'knowledge' thus obtained is contingent on the truth of a non-falsifiable claim. Second, this presupposition flies in the face of the most basic facts that everyone knows about human action. It is one thing to suppose that atoms of hydrogen and oxygen do not make choices, and that they therefore always combine in the same way to produce water, but it is difficult if not entirely implausible to make the same supposition in respect to human beings. Last, but not least, this approach turns out to be downright contradictory once we apply it to the actions of scholar-economists. For what about explaining what *they* do? One would need to come up with a theory and with predictions of what they are going to discover and how their acts will be altered accordingly. But this involves a contradiction with the very meaning of scientific research, which is that scholars can learn something from their tests, something that is not known beforehand.

A very short introduction to Austrian economics

These criticisms of the positivistic approach in economics are fairly widely known. Austrians do not hold a monopoly knowledge about the methodological and epistemological shortcomings of today's mainstream economics. What distinguishes the Austrians is the way they work forward from these criticisms. Indeed, among those who are aware that positivism is an impasse for the social sciences, two general attitudes have prevailed. The first is to conclude that whatever economics is, it cannot be science. Maybe it is a rhetoric, maybe an art, maybe an idle con-game, but it cannot provide any reliable knowledge about the causes and effects of human action. Austrians disagree. They think the right way out of the positivistic quagmire is to identify and use other, better methods. They build on the approach that prevailed before the positivistic approach became dominant, inherited from the 'realist' tradition in philosophy.

Recall that in the course of criticising the mainstream method, we made some claims about action and choice. In fact, the starting point of Austrian theorising is what has been called the 'axiom of action', that humans act and that action is the purposive employment of chosen means to reach chosen ends, as when people decide to spend their money on this book (means) in order to learn something new (an end) instead of doing something else. This starting point is self-evident in the sense that it cannot be denied without contradiction. Any attempt to refute it would involve a choice and would use (argumentative) means to attain its objective. Thus the axiom is undeniable, non-falsifiable, and certainly tells us something about the real world.

Austrian economists use the same method of logical inference in order to identify *universal* causes and consequences of human action in all sorts of empirical contexts.

They always try to deduce such necessary causal relations from the structural features of human action. The truth of these deductions does not need testing and, in fact, cannot be tested for the aforementioned reasons. As long as they are derived according to the laws of logic, they are as true as the starting point. Thus the theoretical edifice built on those grounds is a 'logic of action' or, as Ludwig von Mises coined it, 'praxeology'.

So how do Austrians deal with *contingent* causal relationships, i.e. those relationships which are dependent on other factors, such as those resulting in the determination of a particular price for some barrel of oil last month (which could have been different)? They hold that these require a different 'historical' method, namely, the psychological understanding of the singular motivations that prompt this or that act in this or that context. The interpretation of the real world always involves both types of tools: universal laws and contingent historical understanding.

Let us illustrate praxeological (deductive) analysis of the structural features of human action with a few more basic examples. We already said that human action always involves using means to attain ends, such as picking this book in order to learn something. Now consider the nature of means, also known as 'economic goods'. Such goods have certain structural features; otherwise, they would not and could not be used in human action. For example, this book must be known to exist and must be thought to be useful to attain certain goals. As an inanimate object, it is also easily controllable or 'ownable'. It could not be used as a means otherwise. And goods must be scarce; that is, the available quantity of a good must be insufficient to meet all ends that depend on it. You cannot read this copy and wedge a piece of furniture with it simultaneously, and someone else cannot burn it while you are enjoying reading it. Also, it did not end up in your hands through mere force of will: it had to be somehow produced through the use of other scarce means. This latter characteristic of scarcity is at the heart of human action and of economic analysis. Without scarcity, consumers' goods would be available in superabundance. There would then be almost no necessity to make any choice and, in fact, no need to produce anything. Human action as we know it would simply not exist.

The necessity of choosing requires the ranking in order of preference of those different uses in relation to the ends deemed priorities. In acting, one tries to bring about a state of affairs preferred to some others that could have occurred if the choice had been different. Also, valuation and decisions are made 'on the margin'. An acting person does not rank the satisfaction he or she could derive from some use over another of the whole stock of a good available in the world, such as water in general, but of those units, each one valued separately, that he or she could use in a concrete act. If I can use only two litres of water today but would require 30 litres in order to fulfill all the goals I can pursue with water as a means, I cannot avoid deciding if bathing the cat is a priority or not, for instance. If I am considering acquiring a third litre of water today, I then only make a valuation of the needs which are not already fulfilled with the first two litres, i.e. if I have already bathed the cat, I will not include this in my ranking of priorities of what do with the third litre of water. The next best reachable uses then provide me with the 'marginal utility' of water in this context, that I weigh against the satisfaction or utility that I could derive from other states of affairs which I could bring about instead, say, by buying some food instead of water.

Let us throw our spotlight on another structural feature of human action: its relationship to time. Action is always oriented to improve the future, and this future improvement must be uncertain from the point of view of the acting person. The improvement must depend on his or her action (among other factors); otherwise, he or she would not act at all. These facts are at the heart of basic economic concepts such as 'entrepreneurship' and 'time preference'.

Whoever is faced with an uncertain future necessarily engages in entrepreneurship. Not all people are capitalist-entrepreneurs who invest their monetary savings, but all students are labourer-entrepreneurs who invest their time and labour to prepare for a future professional life in a world of uncertainty.

Whoever wishes to live in the future must survive the present. If one did not have to care for the present, one could spend all of one's time with life's most rewarding activities, the kind of activities we prefer in and for themselves, such as learning philosophy and foreign languages, and contemplating the beauty of nature. But such activities have two things in common: they absorb a lot of time and they do not put any bread on the table. To make it through the present, it is necessary to give priority to present consumption over future consumption, other things held constant. This necessity is known as time preference. In the standard textbooks, this present orientedness is portrayed as an unnecessary but usual feature of human action. Austrian economists usually conceive it as a necessary feature of action. Even people who, in their thoughts, care only about the future must give preference to present want satisfaction in practice, if they want to reach the world of their dreams. As a consequence, they may sacrifice present satisfaction but only if it allows them to obtain more consumer goods per unit of time in the future. Most notably, less present consumption makes it possible to invest the saved resources in more time-consuming and physically productive processes of production, through the building of 'capital goods' (i.e. machines and other produced devices which, in combination with labour and land sites, help produce the consumer goods that directly serve human needs).

Consider a final example for a structural feature of human action, this time involving the social dimension of action. As known since David Ricardo at least, production for exchange exists because each participant can expect to benefit from the higher productivity of the division of labour (coordination). For instance, if person A can produce 1 kg of food or 1 cloth per day while person B can produce 3 kgs of food or 2 clothes per day, and A specialises in the production of clothes while B specialises in the production of food, they can both benefit from specialisation and exchange at a price between 1 kg and 1.5 kg of food per cloth, say 1.3 kg, insofar as they are interested in both goods as consumers. Indeed, at this price A gets more food for 1 cloth than in isolation, when she must sacrifice 1 cloth to get only 1 kg of food. And B must give up less food for one cloth than under isolation (1.3 kg instead of 1.5).

However, human interaction can result in conflicts over decision-making power in coordinating production and over the use of the available consumers' goods. Such conflicts can be resolved, or at least be minimised, by instituting private-property rights on economic goods. This is why, historically, such private-property rights can be found in civilisations all over the world. Accordingly, they play a central role in economic analysis, and in Austrian economics in particular. Austrians stress that different ways to acquire property (appropriation regimes) tend to entail different consequences. Fundamentally, they distinguish (A) the acquisition of property based on the consent of the previous owner from (B) the acquisition of property based on the coercion of, or threat of coercion against, the previous owner. The classic case of (A) is a market exchange. The classic case of (B) is a government intervention. One basic difference between (A) and (B) is that, in a market exchange, both parties expect to benefit; otherwise, the exchange would not take place at all, whereas when coercion enters the picture, only the aggressor expects to benefit, and the victims presumably do not.

Other differences depend on the type of coercion that is involved. Here it is useful to distinguish between repressive and permissive interventions. Governments can over-rule the will of present property owners by forcing them to do things that they would not have done voluntarily, such as paying taxes, respecting regulations, and refraining from selling heroin (repressive interventions). But they can also enable certain people (or everyone) to overstep the boundaries of their own private property, for example, by paying them subsidies and by allowing them to break contracts (permissive interventions).

Repressive interventions are best known, both in the Austrian and in the mainstream literature. The classic examples are maximum buying prices and minimum selling prices. Here the Austrian analysis is similar to what mainstream microeconomics tells us in that a maximum buying price for a good below its free market clearing price makes a shortage of the good under consideration unavoidable and a minimum selling price below the free market clearing price for another good or service makes a surplus unavoidable (forced unemployment in the case of labour). Now the specific Austrian contribution, developed in particular by Mises, is that such price-control policies are not sustainable if pursued consistently.

Given a shortage induced by enacting a 'maximum price', for instance – unless it is ready to live with its consequences, the government has the choice of abolishing its price control or of mitigating its impact by imposing another maximum price decree for the factors of production of the good, so that its costs of production fall and the business-people do not run away from the industry. But now the same issue rises again: shortages developing for the factors of production. If the government wants to stick to its price control policy, it must further control factor prices all along the chain of production up until the first stage of the process and make sure they are not bid up in other processes. Maximum prices must prevail there too in order to keep the productive resources stuck in the first industry. Otherwise, they would flow to uncontrolled branches. All prices end up being fixed by governmental decree – the market economy is in effect abolished – whereas the availability of all sorts of goods decreases instead of increasing. Mises offers the German experiment with price controls during World War I as a prominent example of such a development, although the Reich collapsed before its completion (1952, pp. 76–78).

Permissive interventions play an immensely important role in our present-day economies. All payments made by the welfare state and all payments made by central banks fall into this category. In the next two sections, we will focus on such permissive interventions, since they were at the heart of the recent financial turmoil. If Austrian economists have been able to anticipate this turmoil, it was because they had a firmer grasp than most other economists on the pervasive negative consequences of central-bank interventions.

Tools for understanding crisis: government-induced exuberance in financial markets

Most observers pretty much agree on the presence of thoughtless or seemingly ill-considered behaviour in financial markets. Alan Greenspan, the previous chairperson of the US central bank, spoke of 'irrational exuberance'. Financial-market participants have neglected to invest in the 'safety valves' of economic life while trying to maximise profits. This recklessness materialised in a change of the composition of their balance sheet, the accounting device conventionally used to indicate what a firm owns (its 'assets') and owes (its 'liabilities').

The change affected both sides. On the asset side, keeping cash reserves is useful for being able to meet one's obligations when one's income is lower than expected, but it means one misses the opportunity of earning some additional revenue by investing them. Firms that act exuberantly reduce their cash reserves in pursuit of profit. In doing so they sacrifice 'liquidity'.

On the liability side, a firm can finance its activities with funds brought by its owners (equity) and by borrowing money in varying proportions. A higher proportion of equity means that one has more of a 'buffer' to absorb losses in times of trouble, but equity finance comes at an opportunity cost to the owners if the price of debt (the interest rate) is lower than the return of their firm. As the difference between the interest rate and the rate of return is the firm's profit, in that case, the higher the proportion of debt, the higher the rate of return on equity. 'Leveraged' investments (those that are made using borrowed money) therefore tend to be more profitable than 'unleveraged' investments, at the price of greater risks. Exuberant firms are taking such risks. They go into debt to expand their activities or to buy back their own shares.

The consequences are twofold. On the one hand, any given exuberant firm becomes more vulnerable to the vicissitudes of the markets. On the other hand, if many or all financial firms are exuberant, the resulting debt economy makes any one firm's fate more dependent on the fate of any of the other firms. When one fails, it is more likely to make its lenders fail too, etc. In other words, the whole marketplace becomes more fragile, and when one big company fails, contagion can occur ('systemic risk').

Now the crucial question is this: where does the exuberance come from? Most commentators seem to assume that it is just there, an independent variable enshrined into the very nature of financial markets and of financial-market psychology. Austrians beg to differ. They argue that the level of exuberance on any market depends most notably on its institutional environment. Currently existing financial markets are far from being *free* markets. All market participants are subject to the legal obligation ('legal tender laws') to use government-produced money, and such 'fiat money' can be produced with hardly any technical or commercial limitations (since by definition it is not a commodity or a title to some commodity), whereas the money stock of older market-chosen commodity moneys such as gold and silver could increase only slowly. All financial-market participants therefore can expect the central banks to prevent market meltdowns by bailing out the 'systemically relevant' market participants with newly produced base money (bank notes, coins, and deposits at central banks) if needed. Bailouts spread the cost of failure to all money users. Hence, the perverse incentive for the likely beneficiaries of bailouts to take risks on which they would not bet their own money. Hence, the tendency to keep few cash reserves and toward high debt-to-equity financing. Profits are private while losses are socialised. What appears to be 'irrational' exuberance is in fact *rational* exuberance under the current institutional set-up. Or, in the more technical language of economic analysis, irrational exuberance is a manifestation of 'institutionalised moral hazard'.

Moral hazard normally refers to a situation in which some persons are in a position to decide over one course of action or another, involving a more or less uncertain outcome, while some other persons are made to bear the cost in case of failure, against their will. Legal tender laws and central banks acting as lenders of last resort institutionalise moral hazard because all money users are thereby forced to bear the costs of bailouts, in the form of money expansion-induced higher prices (lower purchasing power of money) as compared to the situation that would otherwise have prevailed. Without the bailout programmes that were instigated in the fall of 2008, the euro, pound, and dollar price levels would have declined precipitously and many commercial banks would have gone bankrupt. Thus the purchasing power of money would have increased dramatically, allowing the owners of money to buy bankrupt firms at bargain prices. The bailout prevented this outcome, and the banks anticipated the bailout. This is why in the preceding years they acted exuberantly. They did not have to fear any bankruptcy and any takeover at bargain prices. They knew the central banks would stand ready to prevent that.

The costs of exuberance can also be socialised directly through governments' budgets. After the 2008 meltdown, taxpayers' money was used in the bailouts of financial institutions, which the latter had probably anticipated, too.

It should be clear that the potential for bailouts and the accompanying redistribution of incomes and wealth from the general public toward the financial sector and its main clients is presently at a historical high Fiat moneys are completely unredeemable since 1971, when the US central bank was authorised to break its contractual obligation toward other central banks to redeem dollars into gold. Since then, fiat money can be issued with almost no restriction. Insofar as people realise this (and they do), fiat paper money entails moral hazard on a gigantic scale. Let us underscore that this state of affairs is not an outgrowth of the market economy. Austrians argue that it is a consequence of permissive government interventions in the business of money production, which makes participants more reckless than they otherwise would be.

The government's answer to this problem is regulation. Most notably, banks are legally required to keep minimum amounts of equity and reserves. The problem is that as long as loopholes remain and moral hazard thereby is somewhat restrained in a particular industry, it reappears where regulation is less strict, resources flowing from the more regulated to the less regulated industries. In the same way that the logic of price controls described above requires governments to expand their programme to the whole economy, they have no choice if they insist in keeping a monopoly on money production but to regulate ever more branches, until no investment can be independently decided by anyone without the regulatory bodies' approval. Moral hazard is curbed. However, the reason why the patient is not sick anymore is that he is dead.

Tools for understanding crisis: Austrian business cycle theory

Pervasive fragility explains why financial crises occur, but it does not explain their cyclical recurrence. If one expects local errors to occur all the time under uncertainty, why would we regularly have clusters of errors in the same direction? This is the question that a business cycle theory needs to answer. Perhaps the piece of theorising for which Austrians are best known is their business cycle theory, for which the 1974 Nobel Prize was awarded to Friedrich Hayek.

Mises and Hayek had argued that the recurring busts were the result of recurring booms. The original feature of their theory was the interpretation of the meaning of booms and busts. Schumpeterians, Keynesians, and most other economists felt that booms were just fine, and all one had to do was to focus on avoiding busts. The Austrians considered that the problematic phase of the cycle was the boom, whereas the bust brought relief. In their eyes, the boom phase of the cycle is characterised by clusters of massive investment errors. Misled by artificially low interest rates caused by the governments' central bank–induced growth of the money supply, the market participants invest in the wrong type of projects, which the Austrians call 'malinvestments'. Eventually, these investment errors become manifest in shrinking profits, rising losses, bankruptcy, and massive unemployment. Such a crisis is rightly feared for the hardship it brings to individuals, families, and firms. However, the Austrians argued that, from an overall point of view, the crisis is beneficial because it puts the economy back on its rails.

This is the Austrian theory in a nutshell. It gets more complicated once we turn to the details, so let us just point out the central elements of the mechanism that is here at stake. In the currently existing banking system, mere cash deposits are legally treated as loans to the commercial banks, so that banks need only to keep a fraction of the money to meet the daily request for cash from depositors. As a consequence, equity and money properly borrowed are not the only ways available to the banks to finance loans. They can simply lend money by crediting the borrowers' checking accounts with new electronic entries, and when those borrowers – or the people from whom they buy something – request some cash, the banks gives them the cash provided by previous depositors. This way, banks 'create money' when they make loans, even though there is consequently less cash held in reserve than there are electronic entries which function as substitutes for it ('fractional reserve banking'). The cash itself, in the form of paper money, is produced by a central bank, so any commercial bank operating in the area where the central bank's paper money has legal tender needs a checking account at the central bank to withdraw it or to sell assets to the central bank in exchange for its cash. The amount of reserves that banks hold – cash held plus their checking accounts at the central bank – determines how far the money creation process is carried on by banks (the money multiplier process). The central bank influences the outcome, either by changing the ratio of reserves it may require from the banks, or by lending more or less reserves to the banks, or by buying/selling assets to the public (open market operations), which increases/decreases the reserves held by banks, ultimately backed by the amount of paper money it produces.

When the banking system increases the money supply by lending newly created funds, then unless all market participants anticipate the long-run effects of this credit expansion, the new money depresses the interest rates. Projects which would otherwise not be considered profitable now look like they are. Investment spending is consequently raised relative to consumption spending, as when people become less present oriented, except that this occurs without an actual desire to consume less and invest more (without a change in their time preferences). A growth process is seemingly triggered, with money flowing in stages further away from the final consumption stage, bidding up factor prices there. Stocks and real estate prices soar in the expanding industries.

This is the boom phase. The problem is that without the desire to actually save more, the new projects will be unsustainable. As the owners of factors of production are paid and the new money changes hands, individuals re-affirm their actual preferences by altering their spending pattern toward the original proportions of present consumption versus investment for the future (ignoring here for the sake of simplicity that the redistributive effect may alter that original pattern). So the funds required to sustain the construction of the new structure of production are lacking. The projects are not as profitable as the initially low interest rates on loans had suggested, and they must be liquidated. As a result of a distorted pattern of spending, real resources had been oriented toward projects of secondary importance, from the point of view of the public-at-large as consumers and savers. Eventually the cluster of errors is revealed by losses, business failures, and unemployment. Assuming no further money expansion, this leads to a reversal of the relative price changes which had initially occurred, including a rise in the cost of borrowing to a level in line with actual time preferences.

This is the crisis, or bust, or correction phase. As Mises has put it, it is as if we had a homebuilder thinking he has more resources than he actually has (1949, p. 560). He would then try to build a bigger house than he really can. Not having enough resources to complete the project, he will waste at least some of them if he is under the illusion the plan is sound. At some point, the illusion must end since he runs out of bricks. His error is revealed and the resources he squandered are likely to find a new owner if his firm is liquidated. From now on, business can start again on a sounder basis.

When the crisis hits, governments and their central banks are tempted to stop it, but this boils down to tinkering with the readjustment process. New money creation or public spending to subsidise failed projects amount to an attempt at maintaining the malinvestments which have caused the problem in the first place. Worse still, ever-newer rounds of credit expansion under the pretext of 'anti-crises policy' can create even more malinvestments on top of the previous ones. An Austrian interpretation of the massive bailout plans occurring since 2008 would then be that the alleged cure is actually toxic in the long run. In order to ease pain in the short run, it creates ever more need for adjustments.

The cyclical nature of the boom–bust process is explained by the fact that the institutions which are ultimately responsible for it remain in place. As long as they continue and expand the money supply through credit expansion, one should expect new booms and busts on a regular basis. Since the ultimate cause of such troubles lies in legal tender laws forcing people to use government-produced fiat moneys, nothing but their abolition can prevent future catastrophes.

Conclusion

With its epistemological and methodological foundations, the Austrian approach distinctly differs from all other modern approaches to economic analysis. It can be applied to explain both the causes of the recent financial crises and the consequences of the various government programmes intended to combat those crises. While the Austrian approach is unorthodox by today's methodological standards, its policy conclusions may be considered more orthodox than those of other heterodox schools of thought, in that they paint a picture of pure laissez-faire policies as essential to prosperity, in contrast to pervasive government interventions. However, it should be clear, in light of what we have presented here, that the prevailing institutions and policies are far from anything resembling the practice of genuine laissez-faire, which in the field of money would require the abolition of legal tender laws. It should also be clear that the mainstream theories which attempt to provide a rationale for monetary interventionism in particular are definitely not some sort of classical liberal or libertarian advocacy program. Also, those who think that laissez-faire policies are an outgrowth of mathematical and econometric modelling should think twice. This is not only because such modelling is hardly biased toward laissez-faire policy conclusions. More importantly, the core Austrian thesis essentially consists in a verbal analysis (although attempts at Austrian modelling exist), yet Austrians argue that pervasive government interventions have entailed the recent crises and that the subsequent interventions have aggravated them. They see laissez-faire policies as a path to recovery. They agree that such policies are likely to trigger a substantial economic down-turn in the short run, but they argue that an adjustment crisis of some sort is necessary to get the economy back on track while new rounds of government interventions create additional difficulties which sow the seeds of ever-more-painful crisis.

Recommended readings

Bagus, P. (2015), *In Defense of Deflation*, Berlin: Springer.

Bragues, G. (2017), *Money, Markets, and Democracy*, New York: Palgrave Macmillan.

Hayek, F. A. (2008), *Prices and Production and Other Works*, Auburn, AL: Mises Institute.

Hoppe, H. H. (1993), *The Economics and Ethics of Private Property*, Boston: Kluwer.

Hoppe, H. H. (2007 [1995]), *Economic Science and the Austrian Method*, Auburn, AL: Mises Institute.

Hülsmann, J. G. (ed.) (2012), *Theory of Money and Fiduciary Media*, Auburn, AL: Mises Institute.

Hülsmann, J. G. (2013), *Krise der Inflationskultur*, Munich: Finanzbuch-Verlag.

Menger, C. (2007([1871]), *Principles of Economics*, Auburn, AL: Mises Institute.

Mises, L. (1974[1952]), *Planning for Freedom and Twelve Other Essays and Addresses*, South Holland, IL: Libertarian Press.

Mises, L. (1985 [1957]), *Theory and History*, Auburn, AL: Mises Institute.

Mises, L. (2004[1949]), *Human Action*, Auburn, AL: Mises Institute.

Rothbard, M. N. (2009 [1962/1970]), *Man, Economy and State With Power and Market*, Auburn, AL: Mises Institute.

Salerno, J. T. and Howden, D. (eds.) (2014), *The Fed at One Hundred*, Berlin: Springer.

Woods, T. E. (2009), *Meltdown*, Chicago: Regnery.

4 | Institutional economics

Geoffrey M. Hodgson

What are institutions and what is institutional economics?

Institutional economics can be defined as the study of institutions in the economy. It is now a major sub-field, with important applications to studies of business, developing economies, transitional economies, property rights and much else. It has already had a widely acknowledged impact on economics and other social sciences. Prominent names in modern 'new' institutional economics include Nobel Laureates Friedrich Hayek, Ronald Coase, Douglass North, Elinor Ostrom and Oliver Williamson. An older, 'original' tradition of institutional economics was prominent in the USA in the first half of the twentieth century.

This essay addresses both of these traditions in institutional economics. It must be emphasised that the 'new' and 'original' traditions are both internally highly diverse, that there is significant overlap between them, that some 'new' institutional researchers do work that takes up ideas and themes in the original institutionalism, and that important elements of both traditions are complementary rather than rivalrous.

There are several ways of defining institutional economics, but one is relatively clear and straightforward. Start with the word 'economics'. This discipline has contrasting definitions, including the "science of choice" (Robbins, 1932). This 'science of choice' definition appears in many textbooks, but for most of its history economics (or political economy, as it used to be called) has been regarded as *the study of the economy*. As the great English economist Alfred Marshall (1920, p. 1) put it: "Political Economy or Economics is the study of mankind in the ordinary business of life" and it concerns the attainment and the use of the "requisites of wellbeing". In short, economics is *the study of the production and distribution of wealth and its role in human welfare*.

Now turn to the word 'institutional'. There are important debates about the definition of an institution, but a consensus is emerging that all institutions are *systems of embedded social rules*, even if that definition needs nuancing in some ways and some important controversies remain.[1] Such rules include laws, customs and established norms of behaviour. Consequently, systems of rules such as languages and codes of etiquette are institutions. Money is an institution because it entails shared rules concerning its value, function and exchangeability. Organisations such as states, banks, firms and universities are systems of rules, and hence also institutions. Accordingly, 'institutional economics' becomes the study of those institutions that are tied up with the economy and the production and distribution of wealth. In brief, *institutional economics is the study of economic institutions*.

Note that neither economics nor institutional economics is defined here in terms of (say) analytical techniques or basic assumptions, such as rationality or utility maximisation, but rather in terms of the real objects of analysis – the institutional frameworks of economic activity. Given this orientation towards real objects of analysis, there is the possibility of recruiting insights from other disciplines – such as philosophy, psychology, law, history, sociology and political science – into the study of economic institutions. Other disciplines can contribute to our understanding of that real domain.

The remainder of this essay is divided into five further sections. Section 2 offers a brief history of institutional economics. Section 3 considers some examples of the growing recognition of the importance of institutions in the analysis of economic growth and development. Section 4 addresses the nature and role of the individual and his or her motivations. Section 5 discusses property rights, the role of law and transaction costs. Section 6 concludes the essay with some brief remarks on the development of institutional economics in the future.

A brief history of institutional economics

The original institutional economics existed in the United States in the first half of the twentieth century. It was inspired by Thorstein Veblen, Wesley C. Mitchell, John R. Commons and other American economists. For a while this earlier tradition was pervasive in leading American universities and research institutes (Rutherford, 2001, 2011; Hodgson, 2004). Even after World War II, the original institutionalism retained some influence. For example, the popular and prolific writer John Kenneth Galbraith synthesised original institutionalist and Keynesian views. The economists Simon Kuznets (originally from Belarus but became a US citizen) and Gunnar Myrdal (from Sweden) were aligned to the original institutionalism and they won Nobel Prizes in 1971 and 1974, respectively. The American Nobel Laureates Elinor Ostrom (2004), Herbert Simon (1979, p. 499) and Oliver Williamson (1975, pp. 3, 254; 1985, pp. 3–5) have all reported that they were influenced by Commons in particular.

A common theme in the original institutionalism, from the writings of Veblen in the 1890s to those of Galbraith up to a century later, is the notion that the individual is not a given, but can be affected fundamentally by institutions or culture. Individual tastes and preferences are context dependent. This contrasts with a prominent approach in mainstream economics where individual tastes and preferences are taken as given, or fixed through life. Instead, original institutionalists emphasize how people are affected by culture and institutions, and can develop different preferences. For instance, Veblen (1909, p. 629) wrote of the "wants and desires, the end and aim, the ways and the means . . . of the individual's conduct" being affected by changing institutional circumstances. Similarly, the American institutional economist Clarence Ayres (1944, p. 84) explained: " 'wants' are not primary. . . . They are social habits. For every individual their point of origin is in the mores of his community".

The idea that individual tastes and preferences are not given, but are shaped by institutional or cultural circumstances, and by particular influences such as advertising, is also a major theme in the writings of Galbraith. For instance, Galbraith (1969, p. 152) insisted that individual "wants can be synthesised by advertising, catalysed by salesmanship, and shaped by the discreet manipulations of the persuaders". Advertising is often more than mere information: it can subtly alter our preferences.

This does not imply a neglect of individual power or agency. Veblen and Commons recognised that individuals create and change institutions, just as institutions mould and constrain individuals (Hodgson, 2004).[2] The original institutionalism is not necessarily confined to a 'top-down' view where every individual is seen simply as a reflection of cultural or institutional circumstances. Veblen and others recognised that individuals differ from one another, even in one culture, and that they are active and creative agents.

The original institutionalism was diverse and varied. Its practitioners worked on a variety of topics, from microeconomics to macroeconomics, influencing labour economics, industrial economics, agricultural economics, development economics, public policy, the study of business cycles, national income accounting, macroeconomic policy and much else.

Before 1930 there was relatively little mathematics in economics. Thereafter, economists became increasingly persuaded about the importance of mathematics. Mathematics is an important tool, but the kind of mathematics adopted tended to squeeze out institutional analysis.

For example, instead of a detailed examination of the institutional structure of the firm, economists began to treat it simply as a 'production function' (a mathematical function such as $Q = f(K, L)$, relating inputs such as capital and labour to outputs). This was deemed to be sufficient to model the process of production, at both the firm and national levels.

In this vein, economists developed an approach described as 'growth accounting'. Using aggregate data on economic growth, and assuming standard production functions, attempts were made to attribute the growth over time as a consequence of changes in the inputs of capital or labour. One of the seminal contributions in this genre was by Robert Solow (1957). But this and subsequent studies found that measured capital and labour could not account for a large part of the economic growth. At the time it was argued that this unexplained residual was due to technological change, but there was no adequate and independent measure of technology to confirm this view.

A group of economists suggested that institutions should be re-introduced into the picture. For example, in an influential paper studying the historical growth of international maritime trade from the seventeenth to the nineteenth century, Douglass North (1968) argued that technological change was not the preeminent driver of increased productivity that many economic historians had claimed. More important was the reduction in piracy, the development of a few large ports, and the growth of larger, more organised markets. These developments were related to more effective political, military and legal institutions, and they helped explain much of the productivity gains since 1600.

Mancur Olson (1982) also brought empirical data on institutions into the explanation of economic growth. By that time, Oliver Williamson (1975) had advanced the analysis of the institutional structure of the firm, and North (1981) and others had showed the importance of institutions in understanding the rise of modern economies. After an almost-complete absence of about half a century, institutions were firmly back on the agenda.

Coase, North and Williamson described themselves as 'new institutional economists'. They brought in new ideas, such as the concept of 'transaction costs': these are broadly defined as the costs of negotiating and enforcing contracts. Transaction costs were shown to be of major significance in our understanding of the role of institutions.

Institutional economists do not reject the use of mathematics but focus on complex, relational and qualitative phenomena that are often difficult to model mathematically. This means that institutional economics is generally less mathematical than mainstream economics, although some institutional economists now make extensive use of tools such as game theory, agent-based modelling and econometrics.

A more detailed look at both the original and new institutionalisms shows that while they were historically distinctive and products of their times, they have been both highly internally varied and often evolving schools of thought. Consequently, there is some overlap between ideas in the two traditions. The theoretical boundaries between the 'old' and the 'new' institutionalism have become less distinct (Dequech, 2002; Hodgson, 2004, 2014).

In addition, there is a wide divergence of policy views among institutional economists, including within both the 'original' and 'new' camps. Among themselves, institutional economists disagree widely on the question of the best amount of state intervention in the economy and on the optimal extent of market regulation. Institutional economics is not defined in terms of a particular policy approach, although it does always pay attention to the role of institutions.

Institutional economics and economic development

To illustrate how institutional factors can affect economic growth, consider the case of growth in China. China began to grow rapidly when it introduced market reforms after 1978. But after spectacular economic expansion from 1980 to 2015, with average growth rates around 9 per cent per annum, there is now clear evidence of a slowdown, with current rates of GDP growth around 6 per cent per annum. How can this slowdown be explained?

Some prominent models predict long-continuing rapid growth. Many of these studies use standard production functions. Most optimistically, Nobel Laureate Robert Fogel (2010) predicted that China's GDP will grow at an average rate of about 8 per cent until 2040, by which time its GDP per capita would be twice that of Europe and similar to that of the USA. But China's GDP growth is already well below Fogel's forecast. The production function approach has limitations because it generally sidelines institutions. It does not take into account the kind of institutional changes that are needed to bring China into the range of middle-income countries.

Examination of the institutional transformations required to develop China further suggest that there are structural and institutional difficulties in the way. Unless overcome, they are likely to cause a further growth slowdown. China has acknowledged institutional problems in several areas, including national political governance, corporate law, property law, finance and land tenure (Hodgson and Huang, 2013). China has yet to develop a modern legal system that is sufficiently independent from political interference. The security of private enterprise depends on this. Land is largely owned by local collectives, limiting the legal rights of farmers to control or sell the land that they have been allocated. Although it is very difficult to develop a predictive model using institutional variables, institutional analysis can highlight important areas where institutional changes are needed.

Accordingly, Daron Acemoglu and James Robinson (2012, p. 442) argued that big changes in China's political institutions will be required to sustain future growth. In particular, a more pluralist political system will be required, with adequate countervailing power. This could help to make the legal system much more independent, so that it is more able to protect citizens and corporations from arbitrary confiscations by the state.

The division of Korea into North and South after 1953 also illustrates the importance of institutions. In 1960 the two halves of Korea were at a similar level of development. The North adopted Communist central planning and the South a mixed system of private and public enterprise. By 2010 GDP per capita in the South was about 17 times greater than that in the North. Daron Acemoglu et al. (2005) pointed out that the two Koreas do not differ greatly in terms of resources, culture or climate, yet growth in the South has greatly exceeded that in the Communist North. A major explanation for this divergence must be the differences in economic institutions.

Acemoglu and his colleagues have also suggested that different forms of colonialism have led to very different economic outcomes. On the one hand, in North America, Australia and a few other places, the British colonisers made a deliberate attempt to set up legal and governmental institutions similar to those in their homeland. British laws and political institutions were copied and modified. On the other hand, Britain and other European colonisers in Africa and South America, partly for reasons of disease in the tropical climate, were less inclined to build up European institutions that are conducive to development. The colonisers focused instead on the (often brutal) extraction of slaves and raw materials. According to Acemoglu et al. (2005), these different founding institutions largely explain subsequent divergence of economic performance.

Acemoglu and Robinson (2012) also pointed to the vivid example of the city of Nogales, which is cut in half by the border between the USA and Mexico. They noted the spectacular differences in average income, education, and health between the two parts of the divided city. They explained this in terms of the different political and legal institutions in the two countries. In Mexico the legal system is more corrupt and less efficient and hence less able to enforce contracts and protect property.

There is now widespread recognition that institutions are major factors in helping to explain economic development. This has opened up a large arena of empirical research and policy discussion.

Institutional economics, the individual and individual motivation

Mainstream economists often assume that the individual acts like a rational calculator, maximising his or her own utility (or satisfaction). By contrast, most leading institutional economists – including Veblen, Commons, Coase, North and Williamson – have emphasised that the individual has limited information and is often unable to appraise the optimal position.

Important here is the idea of 'bounded rationality' as developed by Herbert Simon (1957, 1979). He argued that individual rationality is 'bounded' because of limited information or limited capacity to analyse highly complex situations or problems. Among others, North and Williamson both emphasised bounded rationality.

But in other respects there are differences among institutional economists on how they understand individual motivation. Veblen (1899) notably emphasised habits. These are formed through repetition of action or thought. They are influenced by prior activity and have durable, self-sustaining qualities. But contrary to some popular formulations, habit here does not mean behaviour. It is a *propensity* to behave in particular ways in a particular class of situations (Camic, 1986; Ouellette and Wood, 1998; Wood et al., 2002).

A habit may exist even if it is not manifest in behaviour. Habits are potential behaviours, and they can be triggered by an appropriate stimulus or context. Our knowledge of a language, or a skill like riding a bicycle, is embedded into our habits and is triggered by specific circumstances. These ingrained habits do not dominate our behaviour all the time.

By contrast, some mainstream economists see habit as regular behaviour – rather than a propensity – and then try to explain it as a utility-maximising individual making repeatedly similar choices. By contrast, the Veblenian approach regards habits, rather than choice, as primary: the capacity to choose, and to reason about choices, comes *after* the formation of crucial habits of cognition, thought or behaviour (Hodgson, 2004).

The Veblenian concept of habit points to a crucial psychological mechanism by which institutions may affect individuals. Insofar as individuals are constrained or motivated to follow particular institutional norms or rules, they tend to strengthen habits that are consistent with this behaviour. They may then rationalise these outcomes in terms of preference or choice (Hodgson, 2010; Hodgson and Knudsen, 2004). According to this view, conscious choices are generally the outcome of habits, rather than the other way around.

Other institutional economists pay less attention to underlying psychological processes, focusing principally on the choosing actor and his or her information and incentives. Examples here include Coase's (1937) and Williamson's (1975, 1985) transaction cost analysis of the firm and Schotter's (1981) game-theoretic analysis of institutions. Generally these newer approaches do not probe the possibility that individual preferences or capabilities may be moulded or changed by different institutional circumstances (Hodgson and Knudsen, 2004, 2007).

But North (1981, 1990, 1994) was increasingly an exception, as he delved further into how ideologies and other cognitive factors can frame our thoughts and preferences, in specific institutional and cultural environments. He pointed to the limits of the standard rational-choice framework. He wrote: "History demonstrates that ideas, ideologies, myths, dogmas and prejudices matter; and an understanding of the way they evolve is necessary. . . . Belief structures get transformed into societal and economic structures by institutions" (North, 1994, pp. 362–363). This recognition of social influences on individual cognition placed North very close to the original institutionalists (Groenewegen et al., 1995, Rutherford, 1995).

The starting point of a *given* individual (with fixed and enduring tastes and preferences) is problematic. It could be a temporary explanatory simplification, but ultimately we need to probe further. Individual choice requires a conceptual framework to make sense of the world. The reception of information by individuals requires cognitive norms and frames to process and make sense of that information. As the original institutionalists argued, the transmission of information from individual to individual is impossible without immersion in a common culture, in which the individual learns the meaning and value of the information that is communicated.

There are also problems with the idea that we can explain institutions *exclusively* in terms of individuals. Even the most basic institutions involve human interaction, typically utilising some kind of language. Language itself is an institution (Searle, 1995; Hodgson, 2006). The communication of information requires shared conventions, rules, routines and norms. Consequently, any project to explain the emergence of institutions on the basis of given individuals runs into difficulties, particularly with regard to the conceptualisation of the initial state from which institutions are supposed to emerge. This problem is recognised by some new institutionalists (Aoki, 2001).

But the stress on individual agency is important. In particular, it points to the role of individual motivation and incentives. But within the new institutionalism there is a difference of views on how individual motivation is understood or modelled, ranging from proponents of utility maximisation (where all behaviour is explained in terms of attempts to increase utility or satisfaction) to those like Coase and North, who adopted a more nuanced view of human nature (which addresses multiple factors, including moral motivation and possible altruism, as well as greed). To understand human motivation there is a strong case for bringing in insights from psychology, as institutionalists such as Veblen (1899) and North (1990) have argued. There is also a place for evolutionary ideas to help explain the nature of human motivation (Hodgson, 2013).

Relatedly, Jack Knight (1992) criticised much of the new institutionalist literature for neglecting the importance of distributional and power considerations in the emergence and development of institutions. Importantly, Elinor Ostrom (1990) emphasised the role of culture and norms in establishing and moulding both perceptions and behavioural interactions.

The idea that institutions help constitute individual motivation and behaviour admits an enhanced concept of power into economic analysis. Power is exercised not only by forceful coercion or constraint. For Steven Lukes (1974), the overemphasis on the coercive aspect of power ignores the way that it is often exercised more subtly, particularly by customs and institutions. He pointed out that supreme power is exercised by orchestrating the thoughts and desires of others.

Many mainstream economists assume rational actors with fixed preferences. This suggests that we already know what we need to know to make choices: our preference function is already fully primed to evaluate options about which we are not yet aware and may not have emerged. But learning increases our awareness of choices and their consequences. Learning is a process of personal development: it means changing our personal outlook and our preferences. The very idea of 'rational learning' is problematic.

Property rights, law and transaction costs

The concept of property rights was stressed by original institutionalists such as Commons, as well as by new institutional economists and those working on the 'economics of property rights'. Property rights are seen as a vital component of the basic institutional structure of an economy with property ownership. But the concept of property rights has different definitions.

For example, the economist Armen Alchian (1977, p. 238) defined the 'property rights' of a person in universal, ahistorical and institution-free terms including "the probability that his decision about demarcated uses of the resource will determine the use." Alchian's definition of property neglects the essential concept of legitimated, rightful ownership. More accurately, it denotes *possession* rather than *property* (Hodgson, 2015a, 2015c).

As another example, the economist Yoram Barzel (1994, p. 394) defined property as "an individual's net valuation, in expected terms, of the ability to directly consume the services of the asset, or to consume it indirectly through exchange . . . the definition is concerned not with what people are legally entitled to do but with what they believe they can do." Again this misleadingly describes possession as property.

The upshot of the Alchian and Barzel definitions is that if a thief manages to keep stolen goods, then he acquires a substantial property right to them, even if, on the contrary, legal or moral considerations would suggest that they remain the rightful property of their original owner. But it is misleading to describe the perceived ability to use or enjoy something as a 'right'. Enjoyment or usage can occur without rights, and rights without usage or enjoyment. Possession is principally a relation between a person and a thing. It does not amount to legal ownership. Rights result from institutionalised rules involving assignments of benefit and duty (Honoré, 1961, Heinsohn and Steiger, 2013).

By contrast to Alchian and Barzel, both Commons and Coase stressed that property must entail legal ownership, and hence the legal system plays an important role in establishing deemed rights. Commons (1924, p. 87) saw the contractual exchange of property as involving a minimum of not two parties but three, where the third is the state or a 'superior authority'. Similarly, Coase (1959, p. 25) saw property rights as determined "by the law of property . . . One of the purposes of the legal system is to establish that clear delimitation of rights on the basis of which the transfer and recombination of rights can take place through the market." By these definitions, property is an historically specific rather than a universal phenomenon (Honoré, 1961, Hodgson, 2015b).

The contribution of Commons, particularly to the interface of economics and law, is still relevant today (Commons, 1924; Vanberg, 1989; Hodgson, 2015a). The role of law is still debated among institutionalists. Some treat law principally as a cost or constraint for individuals, who are simply maximising their 'economic' benefits (Barzel, 1989). Others point to evidence that suggests that many people obey the law because they believe it is the right thing to do, not simply because they fear punishment (Tyler, 1990, Hodgson, 2015c). This raises the role of moral motivation, particularly when following accepted institutional rules (Smith, 1759; Sen, 1977; Hodgson, 2013; Smith, 2013).

Another important area of discussion is the role of law in constituting the modern firm and creating the possibility of corporate agency (Deakin et al., 2016; Gindis, 2009; 2016; Hodgson, 2015a). A key question here is whether the corporation can be treated as an agent in itself, or must be understood solely in terms of the human individuals that make up the organisation. Attention to legal aspects of the firm helps answer questions concerning the nature and boundary of the firm. Hence these questions may help restart progress in the theory of the firm, which has slowed down considerably since 1990.

One of the hallmarks of the new institutional economics is its concept of transaction costs. This was originally highlighted by Coase (1937, 1960) and developed further by Williamson (1975, 1985) and others. Transaction costs have been regarded as the costs of formulating, negotiating, monitoring and enforcing transactions. Coase's (1937) path-breaking argument was that firms exist when the costs of an alternative market-like arrangement are greater than the costs of operating a firm. Instead of organising production by numerous contracts at every stage of the process, the firm greatly reduces the number and complexity of transactions by placing workers in employment contracts under a single authority. That is why firms exist.

But there is an unresolved dispute between various definitions of *transaction cost*, which has important analytical consequences (Allen, 1991, 2015; Demsetz, 1968). Although the concept of transaction cost has been used by Williamson and others in extensive empirical work on contracts and organisational forms, the conceptual underpinnings are still debated. It is difficult to measure transaction costs directly. The many empirical attempts to test various forms of transaction cost analysis have brought mixed results (David and Han, 2004; Carter and Hodgson, 2006).

The future of institutional economics

Institutions are the stuff of social and economic life. Accordingly, the study of the role of institutions in the economy is likely to remain a central topic in the social sciences. In developed economies, the question of institutional design is of major importance. It impacts government policy, and it is vital in the development of business organisations.

The economic development of poorer countries is also a major issue. Institutional economists have already made a major contribution in this area, but there is still much more important work to be done. We need to understand better the ways in which economic, political, legal and customary institutions interact and contribute to economic development.

While many institutional factors are difficult to model, and institutional economics cannot match the mathematical saturation levels of mainstream economics, it focuses on the detailed systems of rules that are involved in any practical attempt to design and implement economic policy.

Other key issues on the research agenda include the following:

1 Many of the successful pieces of research in institutional economics in the twenty-first century have used empirical databases to test various propositions regarding the influence of different types of institution over economic performance. The development, refinement and use of empirical databases measuring institutional features will remain an important activity for institutional economics.

2 Many of the disputes and inconclusive arguments within institutional economics entail different definitions or understandings of key concepts, such as institution, property or transaction cost. More effort should be devoted to conceptual clarification – recruiting insights from philosophy and social theory – to establish more of a consensus and common understanding concerning these core concepts.

3 Institutional economists need to continue to build bridges with other disciplines, to learn from them. Many institutional economists, including Veblen and North, have emphasised the importance of delving into psychology to obtain a deeper understanding of human motivation. The importance of political science is widely recognised, and to a lesser extent sociology and anthropology. We should also follow Commons and others, in paying closer attention to the role of law in the economy. Last, but not least, philosophy has also made a major recent contribution to

our understanding of rules and institutions, and philosophy generally will remain important for institutional economics.

4   Institutional economists, from Veblen to North, understood the importance of developing an understanding of the mechanisms of institutional change. This remains an important unfinished task on the agenda. Institutional economists may be able to make further progress by bringing in insights from evolutionary theory and from the study of complexity.

5   The interaction between institutions and other economic factors, particularly technology, needs to be better understood. While some progress has been made in this area, there needs to be more dialogue and cooperation between the study of technology and the study of institutions. We need to understand the similarities, differences and interactions between these two domains of evolution.

6   While there is no shared policy approach, institutional economists have always had a strong impact on policy. The policy implications of institutional analysis need to be developed, particularly by gaining further insights concerning the nature and role of key institutions such as markets, property rights, corporations and the state.

Finally, the interdisciplinary character of institutional analysis suggests that some effort should be made to set up departments and institutes of institutional research within universities, to encourage cross-fertilisation between different approaches and disciplines. Just as there are well-established interdisciplinary institutes devoted to (say) business studies and technological innovation, academia needs to create space for institutional research as well.

This essay has surveyed the vast and diverse field of institutional economics since its inception at the beginning of the twentieth century. It has charted the growing recognition of the importance of understanding institutions in fields such as economic development. The way in which institutions connect with the nature and role of the individual and his or her motivations has been discussed. Key institutional concepts such as property rights and transaction costs have been highlighted. We have ended with some speculations on how institutional economics may develop in the future.

Notes

1   See Hindriks and Guala (2015) and Hodgson (2006, 2015b) on the nature and definition of institutions.
2   This is especially clear in the writings of Veblen (1909, pp. 629–636).

References

Acemoglu, D., Johnson, S. and Robinson, J. A. (2005), 'Institutions as a Fundamental Cause of Long-Run Growth', in: Aghion, P. and Durlauf, S. N. (eds.), *Handbook of Economic Growth*, Volume 1A, Amsterdam, The Netherlands: Elsevier, pp. 385–472.

Acemoglu, D. and Robinson, J. A. (2012), *Why Nations Fail: The Origins of Power, Prosperity, and Poverty*, New York: Random House and London: Profile.

Alchian, A. A. (1977b), 'Some Implications of Recognition of Property Right Transaction Costs', in: Brunner, K. (ed.), *Economics and Social Institutions: Insights From the Conferences on Analysis and Ideology*, Boston, MA: Martinus Nijhoff, pp. 234–255.

Allen, D. W. (1991), 'What Are Transaction Costs?', *Research in Law and Economics*, Vol. 14, pp. 1–18.

Allen, D. W. (2015), 'The Coase Theorem: Coherent, Logical, and Not Disproved', *Journal of Institutional Economics*, Vol. 11, No. 2, pp. 379–390.

Aoki, M. (2001), *Toward a Comparative Institutional Analysis*, Cambridge, MA: MIT Press.

Ayres, C. E. (1944), *The Theory of Economic Progress*, First Edition, Chapel Hill, NC: University of North Carolina Press.

Barzel, Y. (1989), *Economic Analysis of Property Rights*, Cambridge: Cambridge University Press.

Barzel, Y. (1994), 'The Capture of Wealth by Monopolists and the Protection of Property Rights', *International Review of Law and Economics*, Vol. 14, No. 4, pp. 393–409.

Camic, C. (1986), 'The Matter of Habit', *American Journal of Sociology*, Vol. 91, No. 5, pp. 1039–1087.

Carter, R. and Hodgson, G. M. (2006), 'The Impact of Empirical Tests of Transaction Cost Economics on the Debate on the Nature of the Firm', *Strategic Management Journal*, Vol. 27, No. 5, pp. 461–476.

Coase, R. H. (1937), 'The Nature of the Firm', *Economica*, New Series, Vol. 4, pp. 386–405.

Coase, R. H. (1959), 'The Federal Communications Commission', *Journal of Law and Economics*, Vol. 2, No. 1, pp. 1–40.

Coase, R. H. (1960), 'The Problem of Social Cost', *Journal of Law and Economics*, Vol. 3, No. 1, pp. 1–44.

Commons, J. R. (1924), *Legal Foundations of Capitalism*, New York: Macmillan. Reprinted (1968) Madison: University of Wisconsin Press, (1974) New York: Augustus Kelley, and (1995) with a new introduction by Jeff E. Biddle and Warren J. Samuels, New Brunswick, NJ: Transaction.

David, R. J. and Han, S. (2004), 'A Systematic Assessment of the Empirical Support for Transaction Cost Economics', *Strategic Management Journal*, Vol. 25, No. 1, pp. 39–58.

Deakin, S., Gindis, D., Hodgson, G. M., Huang, K. and Pistor, K. (2016), 'Legal Institutionalism: Capitalism and the Constitutive Role of Law', *Journal of Comparative Economics*, Vol. 45, No. 1, pp. 188–200.

Dequech, D. (2002), 'The Demarcation Between the "Old" and the "New" Institutional Economics: Recent Complications', *Journal of Economic Issues*, Vol. 36, No. 2, pp. 565–572.

Demsetz, H. (1968), 'The Cost of Transacting', *Quarterly Journal of Economics*, Vol. 82, No. 1, pp. 33–53.

Fogel, R. (2010), '$123,000,000,000,000: China's Estimated Economy by 2040. Be Warned', *Foreign Policy*, retrieved from: www.foreignpolicy.com/articles/2010/01/04/1230 00000000000 (accessed 1/02/2012).

Galbraith, J. K. (1969), *The Affluent Society*, Second Edition, London: Hamilton.

Gindis, D. (2009), 'From Fictions and Aggregates to Real Entities in the Theory of the Firm', *Journal of Institutional Economics*, Vol. 5, No. 1, pp. 25–46.

Gindis, D. (2016), 'Legal Personhood and the Firm: Avoiding Anthropomorphism and Equivocation', *Journal of Institutional Economics,* Vol. 12, No. 3, pp. 499–513.

Groenewegen, J., Kerstholt, F. and Nagelkerke, A. (1995), 'On Integrating the New and Old Institutionalisms: Douglass North Building Bridges', *Journal of Economic Issues*, Vol. 29, No. 2, pp. 467–475.

Heinsohn, G. and Steiger, O. (2013), *Ownership Economics: On the Foundations of Interest, Money, Markets, Business Cycles and Economic Development*, translated and edited by Frank Decker, London and New York: Routledge.

Hindriks, F. and Guala, F. (2015), 'Institutions, Rules, and Equilibria: A Unified Theory', *Journal of Institutional Economics*, Vol. 11, No. 3, pp. 459–480.

Hodgson, G. M. (2004), *The Evolution of Institutional Economics: Agency, Structure and Darwinism in American Institutionalism*, London and New York: Routledge.

Hodgson, G. M. (2006), 'What Are Institutions?', *Journal of Economic Issues*, Vol. 40, No. 1, pp. 1–25.

Hodgson, G. M. (2010), 'Choice, Habit and Evolution', *Journal of Evolutionary Economics*, Vol. 20, No. 1, pp. 1–18.

Hodgson, G. M. (2013), *From Pleasure Machines to Moral Communities: An Evolutionary Economics Without Homo Economicus*, Chicago: University of Chicago Press.

Hodgson, G. M. (2014), 'On Fuzzy Frontiers and Fragmented Foundations: Some Reflections on the Original and New Institutional Economics', *Journal of Institutional Economics*, Vol. 10, No. 4, pp. 591–611.

Hodgson, G. M. (2015a), *Conceptualizing Capitalism: Institutions, Evolution, Future*, Chicago: University of Chicago Press.

Hodgson, G. M. (2015b), 'On Defining Institutions: Rules Versus Equilibria', *Journal of Institutional Economics*, Vol. 11, No. 3, pp. 499–505.

Hodgson, G. M. (2015c), 'Much of the "Economics of Property Rights" Devalues Property and Legal Rights', *Journal of Institutional Economics*, Vol. 11, No. 4, pp. 683–709.

Hodgson, G. M. and Huang, K. (2013), 'Brakes on Chinese Economic Development: Institutional Causes of a Growth Slowdown', *Journal of Economic Issues*, Vol. 47, No. 3, pp. 599–622.

Hodgson, G. M. and Knudsen, T. (2004), 'The Complex Evolution of a Simple Traffic Convention: The Functions and Implications of Habit', *Journal of Economic Behavior and Organization*, Vol. 54, No. 1, pp. 19–47.

Hodgson, G. M. and Knudsen, T. (2007), 'Firm-Specific Learning and the Nature of the Firm: Why Transaction Costs May Provide an Incomplete Explanation', *Revue Économique*, Vol. 58, No. 2, pp. 331–350.

Honoré, A. M. (1961), 'Ownership', in: Guest, A. G. (ed.), *Oxford Essays in Jurisprudence*, Oxford: Oxford University Press, pp. 107–147, Reprinted in the *Journal of Institutional Economics*, Vol. 9, No. 2, pp. 227–255.

Knight, J. (1992), *Institutions and Social Conflict*, Cambridge: Cambridge University Press.

Lukes, S. (1974), *Power: A Radical View*, London: Palgrave Macmillan.

Marshall, A. (1920), *Principles of Economics: An Introductory Volume*, Eighth Edition, London: Palgrave Macmillan.

North, D. C. (1968), 'Sources of Productivity Change in Ocean Shipping, 1600–1850', *Journal of Political Economy*, Vol. 76, No. 5, pp. 953–970.

North, D. C. (1981), *Structure and Change in Economic History*, New York: Norton.

North, D. C. (1990), *Institutions, Institutional Change and Economic Performance*, Cambridge and New York: Cambridge University Press.

North, D. C. (1994), 'Economic Performance Through Time', *American Economic Review*, Vol. 84, No. 3, pp. 359–367.

Olson, M., Jr. (1982), *The Rise and Decline of Nations: Economic Growth, Stagflation and Social Rigidities*, New Haven: Yale University Press.

Ostrom, E. (1990), *Governing the Commons: The Evolution of Institutions for Collective Action*, Cambridge: Cambridge University Press.

Ostrom, E. (2004), 'The Ten Most Important Books', *Tidsskriftet Politik*, Vol. 4, No. 7, pp. 36–48.

Ouellette, J. A. and Wood, W. (1998), 'Habit and Intention in Everyday Life: The Multiple Processes by Which Past Behavior Predicts Future Behavior', *Psychological Bulletin*, Vol. 124, pp. 54–74.

Robbins, L. (1932), *An Essay on the Nature and Significance of Economic Science*, First Edition, London: Palgrave Macmillan.

Rutherford, M. H. (1995), 'The Old and the New Institutionalism: Can Bridges Be Built?', *Journal of Economic Issues*, Vol. 29, No. 2, pp. 443–451.

Rutherford, M. H. (2001), 'Institutional Economics: Then and Now', *Journal of Economic Perspectives*, Vol. 15, No. 3, pp. 173–194.

Rutherford, M. H. (2011), *The Institutionalist Movement in American Economics, 1918–1947: Science and Social Control*, Cambridge and New York: Cambridge University Press.

Schotter, A. R. (1981), *The Economic Theory of Social Institutions*, Cambridge: Cambridge University Press.

Searle, J. R. (1995), *The Construction of Social Reality*, London: Allen Lane.

Sen, A. K. (1977), 'Rational Fools: A Critique of the Behavioral Foundations of Economic Theory', *Philosophy and Public Affairs*, Vol. 6, No. 4, pp. 317–344.

Simon, H. A. (1957), *Models of Man: Social and Rational. Mathematical Essays on Rational Human Behavior in a Social Setting*, New York: Wiley.

Simon, H. A. (1979), 'Rational Decision Making in Business Organizations', *American Economic Review*, Vol. 69, No. 4, pp. 493–513.

Smith, A. (1759), *The Theory of Moral Sentiments; or, an Essay Towards an Analysis of the Principles by Which Men Naturally Judge Concerning the Conduct and Character, First of Their Neighbours, and Afterwards of Themselves*, London and Edinburgh: Millar, and Kincaid and Bell.

Smith, V. L. (2013), 'Adam Smith: From Propriety and Sentiments to Property and Wealth', *Forum for Social Economics*, Vol. 42, No. 4, pp. 283–297.

Solow, R. M. (1957), 'Technical Change and the Aggregate Production Function', *Review of Economics and Statistics*, Vol. 39, pp. 312–320.

Tyler, T. R. (1990), *Why People Obey the Law*, New Haven: Yale University Press.

Vanberg, V. J. (1989), 'Carl Menger's Evolutionary and John R. Commons' Collective Action Approach to Institutions: A Comparison', *Review of Political Economy*, Vol. 1, No. 3, pp. 334–360.

Veblen, T. B. (1899), *The Theory of the Leisure Class: An Economic Study in the Evolution of Institutions*, New York: Palgrave Macmillan.

Veblen, T. B. (1909), 'The Limitations of Marginal Utility', *Journal of Political Economy*, Vol. 17, No. 9, pp. 620–636.

Williamson, O. E. (1975), *Markets and Hierarchies: Analysis and Anti-Trust Implications: A Study in the Economics of Internal Organization*, New York: Free Press.

Williamson, O. E. (1985), *The Economic Institutions of Capitalism: Firms, Markets, Relational Contracting*, London: Palgrave Macmillan.

Wood, W., Quinn, J. M. and Kashy, D. (2002), 'Habits in Everyday Life: Thought, Emotion, and Action', *Journal of Personality and Social Psychology*, Vol. 83, pp. 1281–1297.

Recommended readings

Acemoglu, D. and Robinson, J. A. (2012), *Why Nations Fail: The Origins of Power, Prosperity, and Poverty*, New York: Random House and London: Profile.

Furubotn, E. G. and Richter, R. (1997), *Institutions in Economic Theory: The Contribution of the New Institutional Economics*, Ann Arbor: University of Michigan Press.

Hodgson, G. M. (2004), *The Evolution of Institutional Economics: Agency, Structure and Darwinism in American Institutionalism*, London and New York: Routledge.

Hodgson, G. M. (2015), *Conceptualizing Capitalism: Institutions, Evolution, Future*, Chicago: University of Chicago Press.

Ostrom, E. (1990), *Governing the Commons: The Evolution of Institutions for Collective Action*, Cambridge: Cambridge University Press.

Rutherford, M. H. (2011), *The Institutionalist Movement in American Economics, 1918–1947: Science and Social Control*, Cambridge and New York: Cambridge University Press.

<table>
<tr><td>5</td></tr>
</table>

Feminist economics

Why all economists should be feminist economists

Susan Himmelweit

This chapter will present what I see as the key features of feminist economics, arguing that these all follow from its fundamental premise: that economics needs to take account of gender relations because the differences in men's and women's roles are integral to how any economy runs. Changes in the economy can affect gender relations and vice versa. Feminist economics is therefore not economics for women, but simply better economics, and all economists should become feminist economists.

Definitions

Although feminist economists have been resistant to producing a list of its key principles and few writers explicitly define what they mean by feminist economics, three definitions are implicit in the type of critiques given of mainstream economics (Schneider and Shackelford, 1998).

It can be implicitly defined by its politics, as economics that focuses on what is needed to create gender equality. It might seem improper to define a field of economics by the political change that it wants to promote. Surely, a mainstream economist might say, even if one is interested in promoting a more equal society, does one not have the duty to be as objective as possible when studying economics? Those who use such a political definition of feminist economics would argue that mainstream economics is itself ideological, based on perpetuating gender inequality by normalising men's lives and ignoring much of what women do (Strassman, 1997). Thus, 'economic man', the typical individual of mainstream economic models, engages in market transactions, supports himself by earning an income from employment and spending the money he earns on buying consumption goods. This individual does not do house-work, care for anyone else and certainly does not give birth. Economic man, therefore, leads a life that leaves out much of significance in women's lives. As a result, models based on him cannot be used to understand, or even notice, many gender inequalities, or to develop policies to reduce them. In practice, of course, such models also provide an incomplete picture of what affects men's lives, since men's existence also depends on unpaid work, on production for direct use and on care, and many men are involved in these activities, too – even though it has been left to women and feminist economics to point that out!

Feminist economics can equally well be defined by its subject matter, as the study of all forms of provisioning, by which is meant everything that human beings need to survive and flourish (Nelson, 1993). The use of this notion of provisioning comes from the recognition that 'the economy' as understood by mainstream economics is an incomplete system, one that is dependent for its continued existence on many activities that lie outside its scope. The survival and reproduction of people and society as a whole requires not only paid employment but unpaid domestic work too, not only the goods and services that are produced for sale on the market, but also those produced for direct use within families and communities, and not only the production of material goods but everything that people need to grow and flourish, including the provision of care. It has since been suggested that "social provisioning" might be a better term for the subject matter of economics, to emphasise that the ways in which people organize themselves to make a living are "interdependent social processes" (Power, 2004, p. 6).

Finally, and this is the definition that I will adopt in this chapter, we can define feminist economics methodologically as economics that recognises that gender relations are a structural characteristic of any economy (Sen, 1990). They are structural in that even if we took a narrow traditional view of the economy, as being constituted by market relations alone, changes in the economy can affect gender relations and vice versa. Causation is not just in one direction, so that any account of the economy that ignores changing gender relations is incomplete. Defining feminist economics methodologically in this way, this claim becomes the fundamental assumption of feminist economics. Of course, it is a claim that needs justifying. However, assuming it is true, then gender needs to be taken into account in any understanding of the economy.

By contrast, much mainstream economics, and also much not-so-mainstream economics, is 'gender blind'. It does not recognize the gender aspects of its subject matter; when challenged, economists will often claim that gender is irrelevant to their particular topic, taking that to be self-evident. Feminist economists would instead suggest that we should *start* by assuming that everything has a gender dimension. It is on this method-ological basis that feminist economics would claim not to be an economics for women, or a branch of economics that studies a particular subject matter, but an economics that by taking account of gender relations is better economics, and therefore that *all* economists should be feminist economists. The rest of this chapter will be taken up with substantiating that claim.

Differences with mainstream economics

In this chapter, I will discuss five main features of feminist economics, contrasting it in these aspects with a loosely defined notion of 'mainstream' economics. The latter includes both neoclassical economics and, with respect to at least some of the features, other schools of economics that would classify themselves as more heterodox. These five main features of feminist economics are the following:

1   It does not analyse market relations alone. Instead, feminist economics recognises that people relate to each other in many other ways, including through relations of love, obligation, domination, power, reciprocity and mutual interdependence within families and communities. The self-centred independent individual, 'economic man', is not taken as the basic model, deviations from which need to be explained, nor as an ideal to be worked towards. The recognition of mutual interdependence between people is taken as both more accurate and a better basis for thinking about improving society.

2   It does not treat the household as the basic individual unit of the economy. Instead, feminist economics recognises that the preferences, interests and choices of members of the same household can differ. Therefore, it is not households who 'make decisions' but individuals, albeit in the context of the families and communities of which they are part.

3   It rejects the notion that people have individual preferences that are independent and unchanging. Instead, it recognises that social norms influence what people want and do, and that these norms change in ways that can be analysed.

4   It rejects a model of work and production that is based on manufacturing as its typical example. In particular, what people do in providing care suggests an alternative model of work and production that is also relevant, to a greater or lesser extent, to many other purposive activities, including much paid work.

5   It uses broader definitions of well-being, assessed at the social as well as individual level, and of infrastructure and investment, that include investment in social infrastructure.

In the remainder of this chapter, I will expand on each of these features of feminist economics. In some cases, mainstream economists have responded to the implied critique (or have even thought of it themselves), but inevitably they have done so by seeing how some assumptions of the basic framework of mainstream economics can be altered to accommodate one or other of these features in specific cases. However, they do not admit that the whole framework might need to be changed, because these features are not just special cases but apply generally. To do that would make them feminist economists!

Analysing market relations is not enough

Feminist economists recognise that many activities that take place outside of the market, in particular the caring and other unpaid activities that go on within households, affect how the economy runs. Furthermore, because people do not necessarily behave outside of the market just like they do within it, the motivations behind such non-market activities cannot be analysed with the same tools that we would use to investigate market relations. (As we shall see, we might also question whether standard mainstream analysis of how people behave *within* markets is correct.)

In particular, mainstream economics' omission of non-market activities means that time spent on them tends to be ignored, or seen as simply 'leisure'. But how that non-market time is spent affects what else people can do with their lives. In particular, a sense of obligation to spend time on non-market activities limits the time that can be spent on employment and other market activities. While this is true of men too, it is particularly salient for women. One of the biggest gender differences throughout the world is that obligations to do unpaid household and caring work structure women's lives and opportunities to do other things far more than they do men's.

As a result, we cannot assume that all workers are wage-workers, and certainly not for all of their lives. While in men's lives non-market activities are often fitted around their market activities, for women the opposite may be the case. As caring and other non-market obligations tend to vary over the course of a life, so typically do women's engagement in labour market activities, giving them employment histories that tend to be much more varied than men's.

This is an example of the inadequacy of taking the self-centred independent individual, 'economic man', as the norm, deviations from which need to be explained. There is a mainstream analysis of household production, known as New Household Economics, which has come up with some useful results, but it works by applying market logic to a non-market area. Its answers are therefore somewhat partial. It can explain why it makes sense for a couple to specialise, with one doing the household production and the other earning an income, and why on average women with greater earning power are likely to spend more time in market work and less in non-market work than those who can earn less. However, it has little to say on any reasons beyond the biological why women might specialise in household production and men in market work. In particular, it has no explanation of why women and men might differ in their feelings about who does what.

Feminist economists would say that such differences between women and men, and their feelings, cannot be explained on the basis of individual characteristics alone, whether of personal character or circumstances, but should be seen as an aspect of the gendered norms of society. Furthermore, because in practice we are all interdependent, the independent individual should be neither the basis of an economic model nor seen as an ideal to be worked towards. The recognition of mutual interdependence between people and their dependence on wider social forces is both more accurate and a better basis for thinking about improving society. So in terms of policy, for example, rather than just enabling individual women to improve their employment prospects by provid-ing childcare so that they can compete with men for better-paid jobs, it would be better to think more about how to organise society as a whole. This could involve making the caring work that women currently do a more equitably shared collective responsibility and redesigning jobs so that caring responsibilities no longer limit anyone's employment prospects.

Unpaid domestic work is not counted in GDP, which primarily measures output that goes through the market. This continues to be the case despite revisions to the system of national accounts so that it now includes the non-market production of food and other agricultural products for households' own consumption (United Nations, 2008). However, as Figure 5.1 shows, estimates from around the world, by one method of estimation, make the value of unpaid work done within households equivalent to about 15% to 43% of GDP (Folbre, 2015). Such unpaid work has become the focus of policy not so much in its own right but because raising women's employment rates has become seen as a way to generate additional government revenue. In particular, within Europe, raising women's employment rates by the provision of childcare was seen, at least until the advent of austerity-driven policy-making, as the main way to fund increased govern-ment social spending (Lisbon European Council, 2000).

There are basically two ways in which the value of unpaid work can be measured. The first is by assessing the output produced by unpaid work and estimating how much it would cost to purchase a similar output on the market; this 'output' approach is used by the UK Office for National Statistics (ONS) for its Household Satellite Accounts (ONS, 2016). The other 'input' approach values the time spent on unpaid work, using either the wage that the person would otherwise have earned (the 'opportunity cost' method) or how much another person could expect to be paid for providing care (the 'replacement' cost method). Mullan (2010) gives a full account of these different approaches and uses them to estimate the value of parental childcare in the UK.

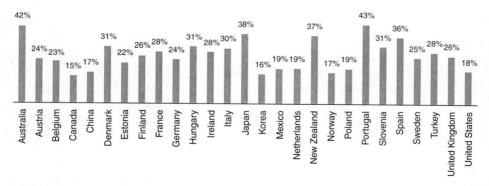

Figure 5.1 Value of household production relative to conventional GDP in 2008 (replacement cost estimates)

Source: Ahmad and Koh (2011)

If we have a view of the total economy that includes all provisioning, it can be growing faster or slower than that measured by GDP. In general, the total economy will not slow down in recessions as much as the more usual 'GDP economy'. This is because some of those who lose their jobs will spend time on unpaid work – to save money perhaps by buying unprocessed foods, or because children are taken out of childcare. On the other hand, when the level of paid employment increases, less unpaid work may be done, and the recovery out of the recession will be slower for the total economy than for the GDP economy (Wagman and Folbre, 1996).

The household is not an individual

Because men and women have different gender roles, their lives differ and so do their interests. People tend to live in a number of different households over the course of their lives, and members of the same household can have different interests. The household should therefore not be treated as a basic unit of the economy into which economics does not enter. Because resources are not necessarily shared equally within households, individuals within the same household can have different standards of living and differing interests.

Mainstream economics tends to short-circuit this complication by assuming inaccurately that households 'make decisions'. But in practice it is people who make all decisions, such as about what job to take, what housing to rent and what food to purchase, to name a few specifically market-oriented decisions. They may well do so taking into account the interests of other members of their household, and may know that they will share the food that they purchase, the house that they rent or the income that they earn with others in their household. But such decisions are actually made by individuals – even a couple's joint purchase of a house involves both purchasers individually agreeing to it.

This is important because it is the supposed rationality of *individuals* that leads to the axioms of rational choice on which mainstream economics is built. But it then uses those axioms to derive conclusions about how *households* behave in markets. However, two individuals within the same household may have different interests and will therefore in general not act as though they had the same preferences. So, even if individuals conformed to the axioms of rational choice, and we will see later why we might even doubt that, there is no reason to assume that households have unified interests and 'act' as rational individual decision-makers.

Mainstream economics does recognise this as a potential problem and has built complex 'collective' models of the behaviour of households consisting of more than one individual. However, although this is a thriving specialist branch of neoclassical economics, it has not influenced much of what goes in other branches, which still tend to take households as their basic unit of analysis and assume that they have unified interests and act rationally. Even Gary Becker, the founder of the mainstream "New Household

Economics" mentioned above, showed this assumption of unified household interests holds only under very particular circumstances. It holds only where a household has one member, its "head", who is sufficiently generous and powerful that it is in the interests of all members of his household to do as he (sic) wishes, because any "Rotten Kid" who does not do so can be "punished" by the household head redistributing the benefits of his generosity (Becker, 1974; Bergstrom, 2008). In that situation, by assumption, all members of the household have the same interests, and therefore the household can act as a rational decision-maker. However, whether or not that model of family life ever held, in many parts of the world today it is no longer reasonable to assume there to be a household head who dominates family life to that extent, and most multi-person households have more than one earner, as well as many shoppers.

So instead of building such clearly out-of-date models, feminist economics recognises that women may not be well served by policies and economic theories that assume unified household interests and equal sharing, or focus too much on a household's current circumstances. This is because women are often the ones who sacrifice their own longer-term interests to those of other household members and may well outlive their current household. Instead, women benefit more from policies that focus on individual well-being and take a life course perspective in doing so. For example, progressive taxation based on individual income rather than family income is generally fairer to women because they pay rates of tax assessed on their own incomes, not on their partners' generally higher earnings. With family taxation, women with partners may find that their own employment brings in too little income to be worthwhile if they need to pay for childcare, for example, but the long-run consequences of being out of the labour market on their future earnings and their pensions can be severely deleterious. This does not mean that women's interests are always best provided for by policies that operate at an individual level – indeed, as I shall argue later both women and men have interests that are often better served by policies directed at a more collective notion of well-being – but women in general do not gain from having their individual interests subsumed under those of their household.

Social norms influence what people want and do and can be analysed

Neoclassical economics assumes that everyone follows the same method of deciding what to do, rationally maximising his or her own utility by making whatever choices lead to his or her preferences being best satisfied. Neoclassical economics generally also works on the assumption that those preferences are unchanging and independent of society. Furthermore, the reasons why people have certain preferences are not to be investigated because these lie outside of the subject matter of economics, which has to take preferences as given. Feminist economics rejects these assumptions. First, people are "humans" not "econs", as the behavioural economist Richard Thaler would put it, and therefore they do not necessarily behave according to this utility-maximising model (Thaler, 2015). But, on top of that, feminist economics criticises the notion of individual preferences as given, seeing instead that what people want and choose to do depends on social norms, whose formation by social processes can be analysed.

Social norms do not fit into the dichotomy between preferences and constraints that the neoclassical notion of rational decision-making demands. According to this view, rationality consists of self-centred individuals deciding to do whatever they most prefer given the constraints of the world surrounding them. In this view, preferences and constraints are entirely distinct and do not influence each other. But social norms are not constraints, because they are not absolute: 'normally' people abide by social norms, but they do not always do so. And social norms are not preferences because people may follow social norms even if they do not really want to, possibly because they think they should or because they fear social disapproval if they don't.

One way to put this is that individuals are not the "separative selves" that neoclassical economics claims, with a clear, well-defined boundary between the self and the outside world (England, 2003). Feminist economists recognise that who we are, how we choose and what we do are not in practice determined simply by a person's individual characteristics facing the constraints of a completely external world. Rather, social norms *both* define who we are and limit what we can choose.

And this is not just a case of one-way causation. Social norms are influenced by what people do. For example, up until the 1990s, the attitudes toward mothers of small children being in employment held by both the general public and mothers of small children changed considerably, as Figure 5.2 shows. By the end of the 1990s, less than 40% of the general public agreed that pre-school children suffered if their mother was employed, although in 1991 more than 50% of the general public had thought that they did. The mothers of pre-school children also changed their views. At the beginning of the decade, more than 30% of these mothers still thought that pre-school children suffered if their mother did paid work; by 1999 only just over 20% did.

But the really striking line in Figure 5.2 is the one showing the percentage of mothers of pre-school children who were actually in employment, which rose from just above 40% to much more than 50% in that period. That these changes happened over the 1990s simultaneously with changing attitudes illustrates the positive feedback between attitudes (standing in for norms here) and behaviour. As more mothers of pre-school children entered employment, norms changed and both the general public and, more importantly, mothers of pre-school children became more accepting of the idea of mothers being in employment. This change in turn influenced behaviour, with more mothers taking employment and so on. Such positive feedback makes change difficult to start but reinforces change once it happens. It also makes it difficult to tell retrospectively what it was that started the change.

Such positive feedback between norms and behaviour can also explain why ostensibly similar economies can easily follow diverging paths with respect to any aspect of behaviour that is significantly influenced by norms. Positive feedback also explains why

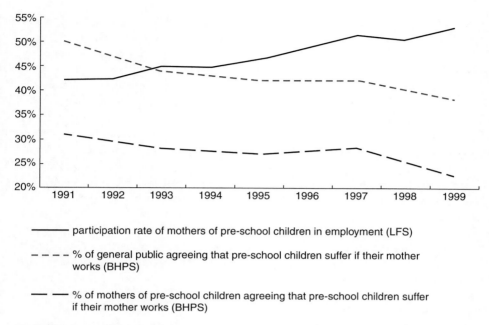

participation rate of mothers of pre-school children in employment (LFS)

– – – – % of general public agreeing that pre-school children suffer if their mother works (BHPS)

— — % of mothers of pre-school children agreeing that pre-school children suffer if their mother works (BHPS)

Figure 5.2 Changing social norms about mothers' employment: UK 1991–1999

Source: British Household Panel Survey and Labour Force Survey (Himmelweit and Sigala, 2004)

it may be difficult for one economy to shift to follow the path of another, because identical policies may have very different effects if adopted in countries whose norms differ. Furthermore, which policies are adopted depends on existing norms, which are in turn influenced by current practices. In other words, because there is positive feedback among norms, behaviour and policy, all three are path-dependent, and history matters in explaining where we are now.

This means that the analysis of social change is more complex than the method of comparative statics used by mainstream economics would suggest. In that method, the effect of a change in an exogenous variable, due to a policy change for example, is analysed by following through the implications for resulting equilibrium prices and quantities. So, for example, a change in the subsidies to childcare, which did occur in the UK during the period covered in Figure 5.2, would be analysed as a change to the gain to employment for mothers with small children, resulting in a higher equilibrium employment rate among that group of mothers. But taking account of the feedback between norms and behaviour would predict either a larger and growing impact on employment or a much smaller one that might just fizzle out. If subsidised childcare encourages a few mothers to take employment, norms should change so that mothers of pre-school children find doing paid work becomes more acceptable, and there is a further boost to the numbers taking employment, which shifts norms further, and so on. On the other hand, existing norms could be so strong that the change in childcare subsidies encourages so few mothers into employment that their effect on norms is insignificant. Therefore, norms make change difficult to start but reinforce change once it happens. Norms alone do not explain patterns of care provision; economic factors, such as the cost of childcare, matter too, but economic change can be speeded up or slowed down by norms.

Care provision provides an alternative model of work and production

Perhaps the most distinctive contribution of feminist economics is its theoretical analysis of care; the hands-on services that children and some adults, according to their specific care needs, require to do what others can do unaided. Feminist economics has placed particular stress on theorising care because it sees the strong gendered norms that almost invariably allocate care to women as crucial in explaining gender inequalities in both employment and domestic life.

Mainstream economic theory and many policy makers tend to treat care as a commodity like any other, whose provision can be analysed using the same analytical tools as any other production process. In doing so they call on a model based on the production of manufactured goods, although claiming that it has more general applicability.

In contrast, feminist economists have shown how care has characteristics that differ from those assumed for the typical commodity of economics. The first of these characteristics is that both the supply and demand for care are influenced by social norms, concerning both people's needs for care and how and by whom that care should be provided, which are highly gendered. Many feminist economists see norms that allocate greater care responsibilities to women than men as one, if not the sole, fundamental explanation of gender differences in society.

Despite this lack of variation in the gender of who provides care, we do find huge cross-cultural differences in who receives care, who gives it and under what conditions. The "care diamond" of Figure 5.3 illustrates the different sectors in which both paid and unpaid care can be provided, some of which is allocated by the market and some more directly by families and communities.

There is huge cross-cultural diversity in the ways in which care is provided. However, like the near-universal tendency to allocate unpaid care to women, some common trends can be observed. As rising industrial productivity has increased the opportunity cost of women's unpaid care work, policies on care to enable women with caring responsibilities to take employment have been introduced in many countries. However, at the same time, there has been an unwillingness by politicians, perhaps reflecting their electorates' views, to devote sufficient funds to provide it fully as a public service. As a result, while family care will continue to dominate provision, the private-for-profit paid care sector is likely to be one of the growth industries of the future. For example, in the UK, a combination of privatisation of care provision and a failure of public funding to keep up

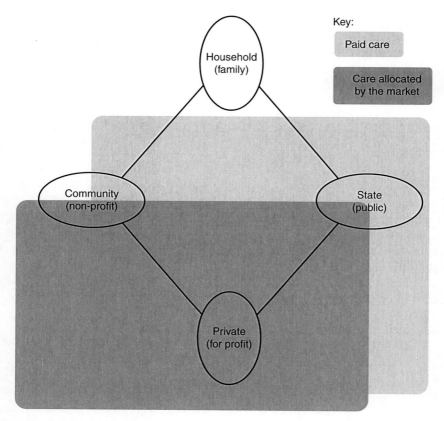

Figure 5.3 The "care diamond"

Source: Himmelweit (2011, p. 263), loosely based on Rasavi (2007, p. 21)

with rising needs has meant that most of those needing care will have to buy their own care from the private sector, rely on family and friends or simply have their needs unmet (Age UK, 2014).

The second characteristic of care that feminist economists have pointed to is that its provision involves a personal relationship between provider and receiver. As a hands-on personal service, care has to be consumed at the same time as it is provided, with provider and recipient relating to each other. This is a significant difference from manufactured goods whose producers and consumers typically never meet and whose consumption can be separated in both space and time from its production. Consequently the quality of the care depends, at least in part, on the quality of the relationship developed between provider and care recipient. Care would be considered of very low quality if the provider showed no interest in the care recipient.

That care involves a relationship between provider and recipient means that raising its productivity is inherently hard to do and potentially problematic. The economist William Baumol was interested in why some industries seemed to increase productivity continuously while in other industries productivity hardly increased at all. The latter industries, which included "health care, education . . . and the care of the indigent", he classified as "those in which the human touch is crucial, and are thus resistant to labour productivity growth" (Baumol, 1993, pp. 17, 19).

In industries of this type, output tends to be measured by time spent. An hour's childcare takes an hour; it cannot be speeded up. In that sense, caring for someone is like playing in a string quartet where neither cutting the number of players nor playing faster can raise labour productivity.

Of course, it is possible to increase the number of children looked after by each childcare worker. But beyond a certain point this is likely to damage the personal nature of care; using less labour but reducing quality is not a real productivity increase. This is because there is a limit to the number of people a relationship can be spread over without affecting its quality. While this limit may differ between different types of care needs, after a certain point spreading care over more people must reduce its quality. Indeed, when it comes to care, measures of high productivity are specifically taken as indices of low quality: a good childcare centre is taken to be one with a high staff-to-child ratio.

This difficulty of raising productivity in care affects the pay and conditions of care workers and hence their training and ability to acquire recognised skills. It means that employers trying to increase profits can do so only at the expense of their workers and/or their customers, by either cutting wages or providing an inferior level of service. As a result, care workers' wages tend to be low, with a care 'penalty' paid by workers working in the care sectors in many, though not all, parts of the world (Budig and Misra, 2010). Although many carers have developed care-specific skills, and are in many countries better educated than the general population, they tend to be among the worst-paid workers and working under the worst, most insecure conditions.

One consequence of the relational nature of care provision is that continuity of provision matters; care workers learn how to care for particular people and are therefore not interchangeable. Care recipients care about who looks after their needs, and changing their carer is a costly procedure in emotional and health terms. Another consequence is that carers' motivations are intrinsic to the quality of care. As well as having other skills, a good carer needs to care about the person she is looking after. This makes the quality of care inevitably hard to measure or evaluate without being part of that relationship. A consequence is that the market does not operate as well as a mechanism to improve standards or efficiency for care, as it might do for commodities whose quality can easily be assessed by potential purchasers and for which changing suppliers has no particularly bad effects. For markets to operate efficiently to the benefit of consumers, quality needs to be easy to assess, and the transactions cost of moving need to be close to zero. This is certainly not the case with care, where both adults and children benefit greatly from consistency of care.

The analysis of care is arguably the most distinctive contribution of feminist economics. Although it was developed to understand the specific features of care, it is relevant to more general economic analyses. In many types of work, relationships are important, quality may be difficult to assess and changing suppliers is costly. Indeed, you could say that these features are not specific to a few types of work, but they constitute the normal case that applies to a greater or lesser extent more generally. If so, then the theory of care is another example of where feminist economics is simply better economics, even for those interested in the traditional subject matter of economics.

A broader definition of well-being, investment and infrastructure

One consequence of the above is that feminist economists have tended to be strong advocates of using a broader definition of well-being, both at the individual and societal level. They insist that existing economic indicators fail to capture much of what women clearly care about, as evidenced by their willingness to compromise their own material standard of living in order to provide care for others. As argued earlier, a more holistic and equitable approach to organising care work in society would benefit women individually, but along with everyone else women would also gain from being in a more equal society that valued care work more. The benefit of living in such a more equal and caring society is not well captured by a notion of well-being measured at an individual level alone.

Feminist economics uses a definition of investment consistent with such a broader definition of well-being. Accepting the definition of investment as expenditure undertaken in order to gain benefits in the future, feminist economics does not restrict those benefits to monetary gain but includes any form of well-being. Thus expenditures on education, childcare and health are investments in the future because their benefits – more educated, better cared-for, healthier people and more opportunities for women – do not just accrue in the current period but last into the future. Such expenditures are also investments in infrastructure because they bring benefits not just to the individuals whose health, care and education are being improved but to society more generally.

In theory, mainstream economics would agree with that, but in practice it tends to restrict the term 'investment' to expenditure whose future benefits are evaluated in monetary terms. This is particularly true of infrastructural investment, which in the international system employed to create national accounts is restricted to physical infrastructure. Thus, spending to employ construction workers to build a school counts as infrastructure spending, while spending to employ teachers comes out of current spending. This creates a gender bias in public expenditure, away from investment in human capital, care, health and education, and in favour of investment in physical capital, transport and buildings. The gender bias is not only in who benefits from the outcome of the investment but also in who tends to be employed in creating it, since in nearly all parts of the world physical infrastructure is likely to employ more men, whereas social infrastructure often employs more women.

Conclusion

This chapter has outlined some of the main contributions of feminist economics. In particular, it recognises that:

1   people relate to each other in many ways other than through markets, with mutual interdependence both a more accurate characterisation of how people relate to each other and a better basis for thinking about improving society than models based on self-centred independent individuals;
2   the preferences, interests and choices of members of the same household can differ;
3   social norms influence what people want and do, and these norms change in ways that can be analysed;
4   the characteristics of care can provide an alternative model of provision to that based on the production of manufactured goods that is also relevant to many other types of work;
5   there is a need for broader definitions of well-being, infrastructure and investment that include the benefits of investment in social infrastructure.

Not only mainstream economics but much heterodox economics would be improved by recognising these features. In that sense, feminist economics is not just another school of economics – and certainly not an economics just for women – but is simply better economics, and economists of any persuasion would do better by becoming feminist economists.

References

Age UK (2014), *Care in Crisis: What's Next for Social Care?*, London: Age UK, retrieved from: www.ageuk.org.uk/Documents/EN-GB/Campaigns/CIC/PDF%20Care%20 in%20Crisis%20-%20What%20next%20for%20social%20care%202014.pdf?dtrk=true [accessed 25/7/16].

Ahmad, N. and Koh, S. H. (2011), 'Incorporating Estimates of Household Production of Non-Market Services into International Comparisons of Material Well-Being', OECD Statistics Directorate, Working Paper No. 42.

Baumol, W. (1993), 'Health Care, Education and the Cost Disease: A Looming Crisis for Public Choice', *Public Choice*, Vol. 77, pp. 17–28.

Becker, G. S. (1974), 'A Theory of Social Interactions', *Journal of Political Economy*, Vol. 82, No. 6, pp. 1063–1093.

Bergstrom, T. C. (2008), 'Rotten Kid Theorem', in: Durlauf, S. N. and Blume, L. E. (eds.), *The New Palgrave Dictionary of Economics*, Second Edition, London: Palgrave Macmillan.

Budig, M. J. and Misra, J. (2010), 'How Care-Work Employment Shapes Earnings in Cross-National Perspective', *International Labour Review*, Vol. 149, pp. 441–460.

Himmelweit, S. (2011), 'The Economics of Care', in: Simonetti, R. et al. (ed.), *Doing Economics: People, Markets and Policy*, Book 2, Part I, Milton Keynes, UK: Open University, pp. 251–307.

Himmelweit, S. and Sigala, M. (2004), 'Choice and the Relationship Between Identities and Behaviour for Mothers With Pre-School Children: Some Implications for Policy From a UK Study', *Journal of Social Policy*, Vol. 33, No. 3, pp. 455–478.

Lisbon European Council (2000), 'Presidency Conclusion', (23 and 24 March), retrieved from: www.consilium.europa.eu/en/uedocs/cms_data/docs/pressdata/en/ec/00100-r1.en0. htm [accessed 28/12/2015].

Mullan, K. (2010), 'Valuing Parental Childcare in the UK', *Feminist Economics*, Vol. 16, No. 3, pp. 113–140.

Nelson, J. A. (1993), 'The Study of Choice or the Study of Provisioning? Gender and the Definition of Economics', in: Ferber, M. A. and Nelson, J. A. (eds.), *Beyond Economic Man: Feminist Theory and Economics*, Chicago: Chicago University Press, pp. 23–37.

Power, M. (2004), 'Social Provisioning as a Starting Point for Feminist Economics', *Feminist Economics*, Vol. 10, No. 3, pp. 3–19.

Rasavi, S. (2007), 'The Political and Social Economy of Care in a Development Context: Conceptual Issues, Research Questions and Policy Options', Programme on Gender and Development, Paper no. 3, Geneva, UNRISD.

Schneider, G. and Shackelford, J. (1998), *Ten Principles of Feminist Economics: A Modestly Proposed Antidote*, Department of Economics, Bucknell University, retrieved from: www. facstaff.bucknell.edu/gschnedr/FemPrcpls.htm [accessed 25/7/16].

Sen, A. (1990), 'Gender and Cooperative Conflicts', in: Tinker, I. (ed.), *Persistent Inequalities*, New York and Oxford: Oxford University Press, pp. 123–150.

Strassmann, D. (1997), 'Editorial: Expanding the Methodological Boundaries of Economics', *Feminist Economics*, Vol. 3, No. 2, pp. vii–ix.

Thaler, R. (2015), *Misbehaving: How Economics Became Behavioural*, London: Allen Lane.

United Nations (2008), 'System of National Accounts', [Online] retrieved from: http:// unstats.un.org/unsd/nationalaccount/sna.asp (accessed 15/7/2015).

Wagman, B. and Folbre, N. (1996), 'Household Services and Economic Growth in the United States, 1870–1930', *Feminist Economics*, Vol. 2, No. 1, pp. 43–66.

Further reading

Agarwal, B. (1997), '"Bargaining" and Gender Relations: Within and Beyond the Household', *Feminist Economics*, Vol. 3, No. 1, pp. 1–51.

Benería, L. (2003), *Gender, Development & Globalisation. Economics as If All People Mattered*, New York: Routledge.

England, P. (2003), 'Separative and Soluble Selves: Dichotomous Thinking in Economics', in: Ferber, M. and Nelson, J. (eds.), *Feminist Economics Today*, Chicago: University of Chicago Press, pp. 33–55.

Folbre, N. (2015), 'Valuing Non-Market Work', UNDP Human Development Report Office, retrieved from: http://hdr.undp.org/sites/default/files/folbre_hdr_2015_final_0.pdf [accessed 9/6/2016].

Himmelweit, S. (2002), 'Making Visible the Hidden Economy: The Case for Gender-Impact Analysis of Economic Policy', *Feminist Economics*, Vol. 8, No. 1, pp. 49–70.

Himmelweit, S. (2007), 'The Prospects for Caring: Economic Theory and Policy Analysis', *Cambridge Journal of Economics*, Vol. 31, No. 4, pp. 581–599.

Nelson, J. (1995), 'Feminism and Economics', *Journal of Economic Perspectives*, Vol. 9, No. 2, pp. 131–148.

Nelson, J. (2008), '*Feminist Economics*', in: Durlauf, S. and Blume, L. (eds.), *The New Palgrave Dictionary of Economics*, Second Edition, London: Palgrave Macmillan, retrieved from: www.dictionaryofeconomics.com.gate2.library.lse.ac.uk/article?id=pde2008_F000286&edition=current&q=julie%20nelson&topicid=&result_number=1.

Office of National Statistics (2016), Output approach to gross domestic product (GDP), retrieved from: https://www.ons.gov.uk/economy/grossdomesticproductgdp/methodologies/outputapproachtogrossdomesticproductgdp.

Rai, S. and Waylen, G. (eds.) (2014), *New Frontiers in Feminist Political Economy*, London: Routledge.

Rubery, J. (2005), 'Reflections on Gender Mainstreaming: An Example of Feminist Economics in Action?', *Feminist Economics*, Vol. 11, No. 3, pp. 1–26.

Rubery, J. and Karamessini, M. (eds.) (2013), *Women and Austerity: The Economic Crisis and the Future of Gender Equality*, London: Routledge.

See also many articles in the journal *Feminist Economics*, which covers a wide range of topics from a critical feminist economics perspective.

For help in compiling this list of readings, the author would like to thank the teachers of two excellent master's courses on Feminist Economics, the first at the London School of Economics is entitled *Feminist Economics and Policy: An Introduction* and is taught by Naila Kabeer, Diane Perrons and Ania Plomien. The second is entitled *Gender Economics* and is taught at the School of Oriental and African Studies at the University of London by Hannah Bargawi. If this chapter has stimulated your interest in Feminist Economics, studying one of these courses would be an excellent way to take your interest further.

<table>
<tr><td>

6

</td><td>

Behavioural economics

Stephen Young

</td></tr>
</table>

Behavioural economics uses insights from psychology to explain how, when and why humans often behave in ways that are not explained by the Standard Economic Model found in most economics textbooks. While some contend that behavioural economics represents a major challenge to the dominance of the Standard Economic Model, others consider that the latter can be modified to incorporate behavioural elements to make it even more robust and useful. Either way, behavioural economics is a fast-growing field with practical applications, which has now moved beyond academia into the mainstream in business and policy, helped by the popularity of books like Richard Thaler and Cass Sunstein's *Nudge*, Dan Ariely's *Predictably Irrational*, and Daniel Kahneman's *Thinking Fast and Slow*. Behavioural economics has grown further in public prominence as organisations like the Behavioural Insight Team, a.k.a the Nudge Unit (set up by the UK Government in 2010 and part-privatised in 2014), have brought ideas from the behavioural sciences, including behavioural economics, to the process of policy making. This chapter reviews some key differences between the Standard Economic Model (SEM) and behavioural economics provides a brief history of the place of psychology in economics, outlines some of the key principles of behavioural economics, and describes how these principles have become influential in public policy worldwide.

Decision making in 'standard' economics

The standard economic model

The underlying assumptions of the SEM, scarcely covered in most economics textbooks, are described by Wilkinson and Klaes in their Introduction to Behavioural Economics. They note that, in the SEM, people are: rational; motivated by expected utility maximisation; governed by selfishness and do not take account of the utility of others; able to assign probabilities to hypotheses (i.e. Bayesian probability operators); have consistent preferences over time and express their time preferences according to discounted utility (normally manifested as a preference for immediate over deferred gratification); and treat all income and assets as fungible or substitutable. Hence, the SEM is populated by calculating, unemotional maximisers, sometimes dubbed *Homo economicus*, who are separated from their environment and from society. When combined, the axioms of the SEM assume away much of human behaviour as studied by cognitive and social psychologists. Whilst the 'unbehavioural' economic agent posited by the SEM makes it easier to formalise economic theory, it is arguable whether it captures actual human behaviour.

The trouble with the SEM: it's not what's in, it's what's out

Nobel laureate Paul Samuelson is often quoted as saying "I don't care who writes a nation's laws, or crafts its advanced treatises, if I can write its economics textbooks". What Samuelson neglected to say was that what is left out of the textbooks can be as important as what is included. Most economics textbooks leave out any consideration of many crucial elements which underlie actual behaviour. The list includes words and concepts such as: altruism; anchoring; biases; bounded rationality, bounded willpower, and bounded self-interest; the endowment effect; emotions; fairness; framing; heuristics; loss aversion; reciprocity; and social norms. These, and many more, are described by Richard Thaler as "Seemingly Irrelevant Factors" for the SEM. Unfortunately, Seemingly Irrelevant Factors include some key elements of human behaviour, all of which can be powerful influences on 'economic' decision making.

The assumption that we are rational decision makers, constantly considering how to maximise our outcomes from minimal inputs while thinking carefully about the costs and benefits of each decision, leads to an unrealistic model in which humans behave like hyper-rational robots. In this world, standard economics finds it difficult to explain many phenomena, including hanging on to things that are no longer useful, buying a lottery ticket, hating to lose more than loving to win, and giving in to temptation. By contrast, behavioural economics takes a more realistic approach and assumes that we are both economic agents and human beings, with all that this means for our decision making.

Decision making and preferences, revealed and otherwise

The theory of revealed preferences, pioneered by Paul Samuelson, is a method of analysing choices made by individuals. It holds that what matters is the actual buying decisions that people make, usually requiring a choice between various alternatives. The economic agent goes through a deliberation process to make a decision, based on what the SEM assumes to be a rational choice. In this conception, our preferences, revealed by what we actually do, are what matter. But the theory cannot illuminate the decisions that people don't make – and the reasons why they don't make them. Enter psychology and Behavioural Economics.

Every day we make decisions: tens, hundreds, thousands – nobody knows how many. Each decision is the outcome of many factors. Some are based on logic. Others are habitual. Most are influenced by context and by those around us.

The traditional concept of decision making comprises the following steps: consider a situation; think of possible actions; calculate which action is in your best interest; implement the action. The third step, calculating the action, is at the core of the SEM, where agents engage in rational calculation aimed at maximising their self-interested utility. Unfortunately, this ignores the behavioural traits that make us human, and which may have a major influence on our decisions. One way to understand this is by recognising, that, in contrast to neoclassical assumptions, our decision making results from the interaction of two systems of behaviour.

Decision making in behavioral economics

Economics and psychology: foundations of behavioral economics

Adam Smith, regarded as the founder of what we now know as economics, saw that humans can be in two minds. Smith, Professor of Moral Philosophy (not economics!) at Glasgow University, is best known for writing *The Wealth of Nations* (1776), but he preceded that with another work, *The Theory of Moral Sentiments* (1759). This includes descriptions of individual behaviour driven by psychology, covering concepts such as reciprocity, sympathy, risk and probability. Although seen as the father of economics, Smith was aware that humans are not rational calculating machines, and his thinking embodied concepts which are echoed in contemporary behavioural economics, such as loss aversion.

Following Smith, Jeremy Bentham, the Utilitarian philosopher, wrote extensively on the psychological underpinnings of utility. Although elements of psychology are found in works by Francis Edgeworth, Vilfredo Pareto, Irving Fisher and particularly, John Maynard Keynes, psychology mostly disappeared from economics with the rise of neoclassical economics. Following Alfred Marshall's (1890) *Principles of Economics*, economists sought to reshape the discipline as a natural science, leading to the emergence of 'economic man' based on a fundamentally rational psychology. This became the ruling paradigm in economics until the re-appearance of psychology, which presaged the contemporary development of behavioural economics.

By the 1930s, John Maynard Keynes was pondering the causes of economic depression and the role of human psychology in the form of the 'animal spirits' that drive investment decisions. In the 1950s, Herbert Simon compared accounts of decision making from economics and psychology, developing the idea that rational decision making is often limited by availability or time, giving rise to "bounded rationality". In the 1960s, cognitive psychology began describing the brain as an information processing device.

Subsequent work by psychologists Amos Tversky and Daniel Kahneman compared cognitive models of decision making under conditions of risk and uncertainty to economic models of rational behaviour, to reveal that actual human decision making often contravenes the basic assumptions of the SEM.

Two systems of behaviour: fast and slow

The 'two systems' model which underlies behavioural economics can be traced back to the ancient Greeks. Plato, in *The Republic*, contrasts the immediacy of desires as short-sighted attractions to particular classes of things, with the broader scope of reason, whose function in the human soul is to "rule with wisdom and forethought on behalf of the entire soul."

Coming up to date, these two different modes of behaviour were captured in the title of Daniel Kahneman's book *Thinking, Fast and Slow*, published in 2010. These two systems, which are critical to an understanding of behavioural economics, are characterised by Kahneman (and others) as follows:

System 1, Fast Thinking: The fast, hot or limbic system is automatic and controls emotions, pain, appetite and sexual responses. We do not have access to this system, which unconsciously controls a lot of what we do, often based on gut instincts and intuition. It is associative and effortless. It tends to be impatient, is orientated to the short term, and serves for immediate gratification. It's your native language. It's detecting that one object is more distant than another. It's completing the phrase 'bread and . . .'. It's answering 2 + 2 = ? It's thinking, 'This turbulence is bad; we're all going to die'. This complicated behaviour has been caricatured as being like Homer Simpson. Or, if you prefer, homo sapiens.

System 2, Slow Thinking: The slow system is the home of cool, considered, complex and reflective thinking. System 2 is the centre of planning, rationality, control and effort, and is slow, patient, self-aware, unemotional and logical. Because it considers the long term, System 2 can defer gratification. It's our conscious thought, our second language, filling out a tax form, recalling a phone number. It's thinking, 'This turbulence is bad, but statistics show that planes are safe'. In System 2, the thinking is complex but the people are not: we make choices to maximise an objective function (usually utility) under the constraints that we face. We maximise our expected utility by assigning probabilities to different states of the world. Faced with a decision, we consider all available information, compare the opportunity cost of each choice, and pursue an activity until marginal benefit equals marginal cost. System 2 thinking is sometimes compared with *Star Trek*'s Mr. Spock, or may be labelled 'homo economicus'.

Numerous studies and experiments show that, in reality, the fast or hot system often overturns the cool reflection of rational economic man. Psychologist Walter Mischel offered children a reward of two marshmallows if they were able to defer the pleasure of eating the first one. Many were unable to resist temptation, demonstrating that our interests are not always best served by our actual behaviours.

Prospect theory, loss aversion and the endowment effect

Kahneman and Tversky's paper on Prospect Theory has become one of the most cited articles in the social sciences. Prospect Theory is a descriptive model of decision making under uncertainty, which uses an objective function such as money or status to capture gains or losses on the horizontal axis, whilst the vertical axis captures the subjective psychological responses of individuals. Both axes can move from their current positions. The theory illustrates not just that there is diminishing marginal value to gains and losses but that it is steeper for losses than for gains – implying that a loss is felt more strongly than an equivalent gain. Dubbed 'loss aversion', this is the tendency of individuals to weigh losses about twice as much as gains, which has been borne out by empirical studies. Figure 6.1 shows that the disutility (loss of satisfaction/angst) of losing $100 is around double the utility (satisfaction/joy) of gaining $100.

Prospect Theory shows not only that humans are loss averse but also that they are sensitive to changes rather than final states, can suffer from inconsistent preferences when the same choice is presented in different forms and are likely to over-weigh low probabilities and under-weigh high probabilities. The implications of Prospect Theory include the following: (a) we have an asymmetric risk appetite – if a choice is framed in terms of a gain, we avoid risk, and conversely, we seek risk if we are in the domain of loss; (b) changes in wealth, whether gains or losses, are more influential than the long-term state; (c) we tend to value a gain that is certain more than a gain that is less than certain, even when the expected value of each is equal; and (d) we will clutch at straws to avoid a certain loss, even if it means taking greater risks.

A substantial (experimental) literature shows that loss aversion, where people place a higher value on what they own, is common, and leads to the 'endowment effect', a reluctance to give things up, even for an equivalent sum of money. Loss tends to be felt more keenly than gain, while we feel the impact of gains and losses independently of final outcomes.

Loss aversion can also apply to beliefs and ideas, explaining social phenomena beyond economics: loss aversion means that it is that much harder to admit making a mistake once we have committed a lot of time or energy to a cause or belief.

Time-related biases

Individuals, firms or governments are frequently required to choose between short-term reward and long-term benefits, inter-temporal choices involving trade-offs between costs and benefits which occur in different time periods. In the SEM the Discounted Utility Model assumes that all of these variables can be distilled into a discount rate, which expresses the value of expected events as a function of delay. This curve is based on the subtraction of a constant proportion of remaining value for each unit of delay, given that, for two similar rewards, we show a preference for one that arrives sooner rather than later. We discount the value of the later reward, by a factor that increases with the length of the delay. This time-consistent model of discounting assumes consistent decisions over a period; i.e. that we don't change our minds.

However, we are as likely to be inconsistent over time, a recognition that our preferences might change. It is as if when making a decision, we have many different 'selves', with each 'self' representing the decision-maker at a different point in time. Unlike homo economicus, homo sapiens has, according to psychologist George Ainslie, a tendency to

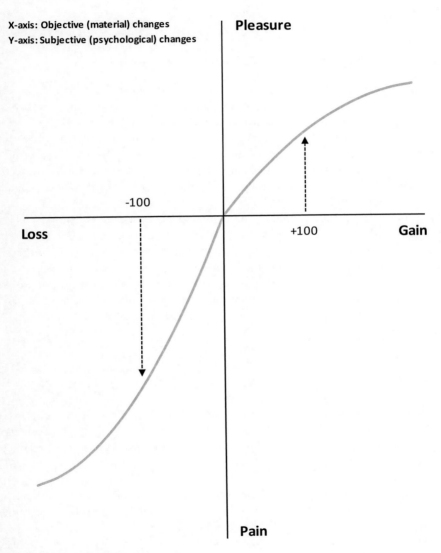

Figure 6.1 Prospect Theory

Source: Based on Kahneman and Tversky (1979)

form temporary preferences for earlier goals, which often offer poorer outcomes. Immediate pleasure gives an instant payoff in the fast System 1, whereas we have to consciously engage the slow rationality of System 2 to defer gratification and calculate the value of future benefits. And present or immediate costs and benefits are more salient or vivid than future costs and benefits. We are largely unaware of this cognitive structure, and hence we are unable to predict that we will succumb to it. So when tomorrow arrives, we might just recalculate the costs and benefits and change our decision. In any case, who knows that tomorrow might bring?

Too much information and too many choices?

In the textbook model of perfect competition, equilibrium is reached at the meeting point of supply and consumer demand. Suppliers in a competitive market are undifferentiated, selling homogeneous products that differ only on price: as no firm has market power, all must sell at whatever price the market determines. When profits are high, new firms enter the market, increase supply, prices are driven down and excess profits are eliminated. If too many firms enter the market, lower prices will drive some to fold, and prices will rise back to sustainable levels. Under perfect competition, no company can make a surplus profit over the long run.

Information is the lubricant for the textbook model of perfect competition – all players are assumed to have equal access to all relevant information, so that prices will reflect all available information. Perfect competition requires perfect information: in the SEM there is no such thing as too much information. The reality is that all the relevant information is rarely available, and even when it is, there are limits on that we can process – we often filter out important details that could end up costing us dear. Humans, rather than econs, can suffer from information overload, which freezes our decision making and can produce bad choices.

As psychologist T. D. Wilson put it:

> at any given moment, our five senses are taking in more than 11 million pieces of information. . . . Our eyes alone receive and send over 10 million signals to our brains each second. . . . The most liberal estimate is that people can process consciously about 40 pieces of information per second. Think about it: we are taking in 11 million pieces of information a second, but can process only 40 of them consciously. (Wilson, 2004, p. 24)

The optimum market structure of the SEM – a multiplicity of players on both the supply side and the demand side – leads to maximum choice and the mantra of empowerment through increased choice. Once confined to economics and the operation of markets, this mantra has now entered political discourse and has become a major influence on policy.

But the proliferation of choice can be problematic for humans with limited time and resources for making decisions. Experiments by Iyengar and Lepper offered participants either a limited or a larger number of options. Whether for jam or chocolates, participants choosing from a smaller number of options were more satisfied and more likely to purchase again compared to those who were offered a larger selection.

These experiments, and similar studies, show that dissatisfaction with choice grows as the number of possible choices increases: people become overwhelmed or indecisive, and the possibility or anticipation of regret can have a paralysing influence in decision making. People may lack the confidence to decide and may choose not to choose, either doing nothing or taking the line of least resistance – inertia bias. This can be worsened when the instinct to avoid regret is greater than the perceived gains from making a choice, leading to loss aversion. As psychologist Barry Schwartz has argued, "As the number of choices keeps growing, negative aspects of having a multitude of options begin to appear . . . until we grow overloaded. At this point, choice no longer liberates, but debilitates" (Schwartz, 2004, p. 2).

While technological developments such as ubiquitous Internet access may be acculturating people to having more information and more choice, ideas around choice overload are now being acted upon by many businesses, including supermarkets: the average British household buys 300–400 products in a year, about 150 of them regularly, with around 40 items in the weekly shop. Limited range continental discounters like Aldi and Lidl have grown rapidly in the UK in recent years, stocking around 2,000 different products, compared with the average British 'Big Five' supermarket, which stocks around 80,000. In 2015, the new boss of UK supermarket Tesco announced plans to pull 30% of the 90,000 products it stocks, in an attempt to cut costs and make the weekly shop simpler.

Heuristics and biases

Whilst the SEM assumes that people will respond appropriately to information that facilitates the effective operation of markets, the reality is that people often lack the appropriate cognitive skills, the required computing power, and the relevant levels of self-control. So to economise on their use of cognitive faculties, people adopt rules of thumb, also known as heuristics, which are mental shortcuts or decision rules used by the brain in reacting quickly to situations. Heuristics work well under most circumstances, but when applied to complex situations, especially ones involving probability, they can produce incorrect answers with systematic errors.

Much of the work of discovering heuristics in decision making was done by Kahneman and Tversky, building on concepts originally introduced by Herbert Simon. In their 1974 paper *Judgment under uncertainty: Heuristics and biases*, Tversky and Kahneman identified three types of heuristics used in decision making which, though "highly economical, and usually effective . . . lead to systematic and predictable errors": (i) representativeness, our tendency to draw big conclusions from small samples, often based on the least relevant data. An example is the *gambler's fallacy*, the belief in runs of good and bad luck; (ii) availability, when we make decisions based on data that we can recall, rather than data which is relevant – e.g., the exaggerated fear of being the victim of a terrorist attack; and (iii) anchoring and adjustment, when we make an estimate based on an initial value that may not be relevant – assuming a sale price is a good deal because it is lower than a 'normal' price.

Framing

More errors can arise due to the fact that our decisions are greatly influenced by how choices and options are presented to us. Although we like to think that we are responding to the information in front of us, we are also highly sensitive to the way in which a decision problem is framed. In fact, the framework in which a question is asked can have as much bearing on the outcome as the actual data being presented. An example is a one-litre jug, which contains a half litre of beer: the same data – that the jug contains 500 ml of beer – can be represented as either half full or half empty. Frequently, our decisions depend not just on the data but on the chosen frame; changing the frame from a loss to a gain can alter a decision, as can presenting the items in a different order.

In one experiment, subjects were told that they were required to make a choice between two types of treatment for cancer. Half the subjects were told: "Of patients who had surgery, 90% of patients survived the treatment and 34% survived for at least another 5 years. Of patients who had radiation treatment, all survived the treatment, but only 22% were still alive 5 years later." The other half of the subjects were told: "Of patients who had surgery, 10% died during surgery and 66% died within 5 years. Of patients who had radiation treatment, 0% died during treatment, but 78% died within 5 years."

What would you do? The statistics are identical, showing that more people survive longer by having surgery instead of radiation treatment. Based on the data, surgery is the right choice, but when the data were presented in the 'survival' frame (first group), only 25% preferred radiation treatment to surgery. When the data were presented in the 'mortality' frame (second group), 42% preferred radiation treatment. This shows that when the possibility of dying during surgery was highlighted, people were more likely to choose radiation therapy, even at the cost of decreased long-term survival. What is even more extra-ordinary about this study is that, despite their training and experience, doctors were just as vulnerable to make the wrong choice as a result of this framing bias.

Behavioral economics and public policy

From obscurity to influence

Public policy was traditionally based on the premise, derived from the SEM, that consumers are rational, use information effectively, pursue their own interests, and are consistent in their choices. Behavioural economics, in demonstrating that individuals do not behave like rational machines, can suggest practical policy and interventions which can be more successful in producing the intended outcomes.

In 2010, behavioural economics moved to the centre stage of UK public policy following the publication by David Halpern, previously chief strategist in the Prime Minister's Strategy Unit, of *The Hidden Wealth of Nations*, consciously echoing Adam Smith's work of 1776. One of Halpern's recommendations for a future Prime Minister was "embrace Behavioural Economics" on the basis that behavioural economics "provides a powerful new set of tools for policy makers and citizens to address the challenges of today and improve the quality of our lives." Halpern recognised that traditional interventions to change people's behaviour, using regulation and taxation, incentives and penalties, plus information and persuasion, may not always work. The UK government subsequently established a Behavioural Insight Team (BIT) with the goal of applying techniques drawn from the behavioural sciences, including behavioural economics. The BIT was soon dubbed 'The Nudge Unit'.

Changing behaviour without changing minds: nudging

Arguably the first book on behavioural economics aimed at an audience outside academia was Thaler and Sunstein's *Nudge*, published in 2008. *Nudge* considered the anomalies between the textbook assumptions of neoclassical economics and actual human behaviour to propose interventions which could be used to improve the outcomes of public policy and produce behaviour change. For Thaler and Sunstein, a 'nudge' is any aspect of the choice architecture that alters people's behaviour in a predictable way without forbidding any option or significantly changing economic incentives. A nudge is "a small feature of our environment, which captures our attention and changes our behaviour." Putting fruit at eye level counts as a nudge, but banning junk food does not. Given that "a nudge can change behaviour without changing minds," it is not surprising that *Nudge* has been described by Daniel Kahneman as "the basic manual for applying behavioral economics to policy."

Nudges, little and large

Nudges are the tools of choice for libertarian paternalists, and they have become the most conspicuous impact of behavioural economics on public policy. Nudges result from decisions made by a 'choice architect', a person who designs the framework within which people make decisions. Everyone is potentially a choice architect, whether it's a doctor describing a range of treatments to a patient, a parent preparing dinner or a caterer designing a new restaurant. The resultant choice architecture can affect decision making in relatively trivial matters, such as whether to buy a particular product, or in life-or-death matters such as procedures for organ donation or arrangements for pensions enrolment.

Pensions are complicated and confusing: people often know that they should be saving for a pension, but they do not get around to setting one up. Behavioural economics has been used to address this challenge, using the power of defaults. A default, what happens if a person takes no action, is sometimes called 'silent consent'. People often 'choose not to choose' and stick with defaults, such as whether or not to contribute, or going with the default investment plan chosen by the pension fund.

Switching the default can have a major impact on behaviour. In one study, Company A changed its enrolment policy for new employees' pension plans from automatic non-enrolment (opt-in) to automatic enrolment (opt-out). With a change to automatic enrolment, participation increased from below 60% to almost 100%.

Such studies have influenced policy in the UK, where the biggest nudge so far (measured by the number of people affected) came into effect on 1 October 2012. From this date, starting with the largest employers, every employee earning over £7,500 is required to be automatically enrolled into a qualifying pension scheme if they are not already in one. Employers must also contribute to that pension, and employees have to opt out if they do not wish to be in a pension scheme.

As the Department for Work and Pensions notes:

> The purpose of the automatic enrolment policy is to increase the numbers of people saving for their pension by ensuring that inaction on their part will lead to pension saving occurring, just as inaction at present leads to no saving. (DWP, 2010)

This translation of principles from behavioural economics into public policy could be potentially life-changing for millions of people. Research published in 2013 by the Department for Work and Pensions covering the 50 biggest employers then using auto-enrolment showed that over 90% of the people placed into a workplace pension by their employer stayed in (previous DWP research with workers across all business sizes found that 30% were likely to opt out).

Behavioural economics goes global: nudging all over the world

Nudge has gone global. A 2014 report by Whitehead et al. noted that centrally orchestrated policies based on behavioural sciences (including, but not limited to, behavioural economics and nudge-type policies) have been implemented in more than 25% of the world's independent nation states. The total list of countries implementing some form of interventions based on behavioural science came to 136. The list goes beyond the advanced western economies of Western Europe, North America and Australasia and continues to grow. Even the World Bank has now noted the rise of behavioural sciences: its 2015 *World Development Report* was on the theme of Mind, Society, and Behavior.

One caveat: there is a tendency, when considering behaviour change in policy and practice, to use the terms 'behavioural economics', 'behavioural science' and 'behavioural insight' interchangeably. As Daniel Kahneman said in a 2015 conference, much of what passes for behavioural economics in the policy field is really "applied social psychology." And as Richard Thaler has commented, these interventions have, so far, used only a small amount of psychology and virtually no economics.

Philosophy and policy: the limits of behavioural economics

Behavioural economics encapsulates a philosophy of 'libertarian paternalism,' a relatively weak, soft and non-intrusive type of paternalism because it depends on choices being neither prescribed, proscribed or made costly to the chooser. Sometimes described as an oxymoron, libertarian paternalism is designed to help people make choices which can improve their lives without reducing their freedom of action: if it's impossible to choose an option that isn't the default, or the designated option, then it fails the test of libertarian paternalism and hence is not behavioural economics – it's coercion, or regulation, or the law.

Some critics argue that libertarian paternalism, by influencing individuals and exploiting their cognitive shortcomings for their own good and for the common good, is manipulative. And who can say whether those who design the interventions ultimately know any better than those they are trying to help? The debate continues on whether behavioural economics is the key to reconciling the traditionally opposed philosophies of libertarianism and paternalism.

Turning from philosophy to policy, it is clear that insights from behavioural economics can help improve the effectiveness of interventions, but behavioural economics alone is unlikely to be able to compensate for structural inequality, economic disadvantage, the prevalence of externalities, or many of the other major challenges faced by society. Problems such as high levels of obesity, alcohol abuse or car dependency are highly complex and not amenable to a quick nudge to change behaviour. Whilst nudges and interventions based on behavioural economics can make a contribution, there will continue to be a need for incentives, penalties, regulation and the law. As Loewenstein and Ubel have noted, "Behavioral economics should complement, not substitute for, more substantive economic interventions. . . . For all of its insights, behavioral economics alone is not a viable alternative to the kinds of far-reaching policies we need to tackle our nation's challenges" (2010).

Conclusions

One question, subject to much debate, is whether behavioural economics complements or contradicts the Standard Economic Model. Some commentators argue that behavioural economics, by questioning the assumptions and axioms of the SEM, is a fundamental challenge to all that is implied by neoclassical economics. Addressing academic economists and students of economics, Kalle Lasn wrote in 2012:

> Outside your department, a vigorous heterodox economics thrives. . . . There are social economists, feminist economists, inter-disciplinary economists, behavioral

economists, ecological economists and hundreds of intellectuals and maverick professors who are openly critical of the neoclassical regime and fighting to overthrow it.

(n.p.)

An opposing view is that behavioural economics, once seen as heretical, has become part of the mainstream. This view gains currency from the flood of publications which are devoted to, or incorporate elements from behavioural economics, which are being produced by regulators, government departments, corporations, marketing and advertising agencies, consultancy firms and think tanks.

Whilst this controversy is unresolved, what is clear is that the assumptions underlying the SEM, predicated on Rational Economic Man, often lead to erroneous conclusions. Many now hold that the SEM takes insufficient account of actual human psychology, and agree that (economic) behaviour is frequently subject to biased decision making and cognitive and mental flaws. Decisions are often based on the hot and fast shortcuts of System 1 rather than the cool reflection of System 2 favoured by standard economics. In recognition of this, Richard Thaler commented in 2015, "Behavioural economics is, to a large extent, standard economics that has been modified to incorporate Seemingly Irrelevant Factors." But incorporating the insights into the Standard Economic Model, or producing a formal Behavioural Economics Model, has yet to happen – matching a model with the simplicity, tractability and applicability of the SEM is difficult if the starting point is, as with behavioural economics, based on a series of anomalies.

The most striking current aspect of behavioural economics is how it is now being used to inform public policy and interventions designed to change behaviour, based on ideas like Nudges, choice architecture and defaults. Although such techniques are now being used by the state and non-governmental organizations, similar insights have long been used by the commercial sector whether or not under the heading 'behavioural economics.' As Richard Thaler says, it's important to "Nudge for Good."

To conclude, what is arguably most remarkable is that economics is probably the only discipline in the social sciences in which the development of 'behavioural' economics could be viewed as what Thomas Kuhn described as a 'paradigm shift'. For practically everyone other than 'conventional' economists, whether social scientists, businesses, marketers or members of the public, the insights yielded by behavioural economics and the contrasts with the findings of the SEM would appear to be little more than 'business as usual'.

Controversy aside, what remains unarguable is that, as Camerer and Loewenstein (2004) say, "Behavioural economics increases the explanatory power of economics by providing it with more realistic psychological foundations." Or as Charlie Munger, Vice Chairman of Warren Buffet's company Berkshire Hathaway, put it in 1995: "If economics isn't behavioural, I don't know what is".

References

Akerlof, G. A. and Shiller, R. J. (2009), *Animal Spirits: How Human Psychology Drives the Economy, and Why It Matters for Global Capitalism*, Princeton: Princeton University Press.

Ariely, D. (2008), *Predictably Irrational*, London: Harper Collins.

Ashraf, N., Camerer, C. F. and Loewenstein, G. (2005), 'Adam Smith, Behavioral Economist', *Journal of Economic Perspectives*, Vol. 19, No. 3, pp. 131–145.

Behavioural Insights Team. Various publications and blog.

Camerer, C. and Loewenstein, G. (2004), 'Behavioural Economics: Past, Present and Future', in: Camerer, C. F., Loewenstein, G. and Rabin, M. (eds.), *Advances in Behavioural Economics*, Princeton: Princeton University Press, pp. 3–53.

Dolan, P., Hallsworth, M., David, D., King, D. and Vlaev, I. (2010a), 'MINDSPACE: Influencing Behaviour Through Public Policy', Institute for Government/Cabinet Office, retrieved from: www.instituteforgovernment.org.uk/publications/mindspace.

Halpern, D. (2010), *The Hidden Wealth of Nations*, Cambridge: Polity Press.

Johnson, P., Yeandle, D. and Boulding, A. (2010), 'Making Automatic Enrolment Work', Department for Work and Pensions, retrieved from: www.dwp.gov.uk/docs/cp-oct10-full-document.pdf.

Kahneman, D. (2011), *Thinking Fast and Slow*, London: Allen Lane.

Kahneman, D. and Tversky, A. (1979), 'Prospect Theory: An Analysis of Decision Under Risk', *Econometrica*, Vol. 47, No. 2, pp. 263–292.

Kahneman, D. and Tversky, A. (1984), 'Choices, Values, and Frames', *American Psychologist*, Vol. 39, No. 4, pp. 341–350.

Kuhn, T. (1962), *The Structure of Scientific Revolutions*, Chicago: University of Chicago Press.

Lasn, K. (2012), *Meme Wars: The Creative Destruction of Neo-Classical Economics*, London: Penguin.

Loewenstein, G. and Ubel, P. (2010), 'Economics Behaving Badly', *New York Times*.

Marshall, A. (1890), *Principles of Economics*, London: Macmillan and Co.

Munger, C. (1995), 'The Psychology of Human Misjudgement', Speech at Harvard Law School, Transcript, retrieved from: www.joshuakennon.com/the-psychology-of-human-mis judgment-by-charlie-munger/.

Oliver, A. (2013), *Introduction to Behavioural Public Policy*, Cambridge: Cambridge University Press.

Ormerod, P. (2005), *Why Things Fail: Evolution, Extinction and Economics*, London: Faber and Faber.

Schwartz, B. (2004), *The Paradox of Choice: Why More Is Less*, New York: Harper Perennial.

Sen, A. (1973), 'Behaviour and the Concept of Preference', *Economica*, New Series, Vol. 40, No. 159, pp. 241–259.

Simon, H. (1957), *Models of Man: Social and Rational. Mathematical Essays on Rational Human Behavior in a Social Setting*, New York: Wiley and Sons.

Sunstein, C. and Thaler, R. (2003), 'Libertarian Paternalism Is Not An Oxymoron', *The University of Chicago Law Review*, Vol. 70, No. 4, pp. 1159–1202.

Thaler, R. (1994), *The Winner's Curse: Paradoxes and Anomalies of Economic Life*, Princeton: Princeton University Press.

Thaler, R. (2015), *Misbehaving*, London: Allen Lane.

Thaler, R. and Mullainathan S. (2000), *Behavioural Economics*, Massachusetts Institute of Technology, Department of Economics Working Paper Series, Working Paper 00–27, retrieved from: https://papers.ssrn.com/sol3/papers.cfm?abstract_id=245828.

Thaler, R. and Mullainathan, S. (2007), 'Behavioral Economics Defined', in: Henderson, D. (ed.), *The Concise Encyclopedia of Economics*, Indianapolis: Liberty Fund, retrieved from: www.econlib.org/library/Enc/BehavioralEconomics.html.

Thaler, R. and Sunstein, C. (2008), *Nudge: Improving Decisions About Health, Wealth, and Happiness*, London: Penguin.

Tversky, A. and Kahneman, D. (1974), 'Judgment Under Uncertainty: Heuristics and Biases', *Science*, Vol. 185, pp. 1124–1130.

Tversky, A. and Kahneman, D. (1981), 'The Framing of Decisions and the Psychology of Choice', *Science*, New Series, Vol. 211, No. 4481, pp. 453–458.

Whitehead, M., Jones, R., Howell, R., Lilley, R. and Pykett, J. (2014), 'Nudging All Over the World: Assessing the Global Impact of the Behavioural Sciences on Public Policy', ESRC, retrieved from: https://changingbehaviours.files.wordpress.com/2014/09/nudgedesignfinal.pdf.

Wilkinson, N. and Klaes, M. (2012), *An Introduction to Behavioural Economics*, Second Edition, Basingstoke: Palgrave Macmillan.

Wilson, T. D. (2004), *Strangers to Ourselves*, Cambridge, MA: Harvard University Press.

World Bank (2015), *World Development Report 2015: Mind, Society, and Behavior*, Washington, DC: World Bank, retrieved from: http://www.worldbank.org/en/publication/wdr2015.

Young, S. (2013), 'The Behavioural Economics of Owning a Car', *eg magazine*, Vol. 18, No. 5, retrieved from: www.globaltolocal.com/eg%2018_5.pdf.

Young, S. (2015), 'The Behavioural Economics of Owning a Car', Economics Rockstar podcast with Frank Conway, retrieved from: www.economicrockstar.com/stephenyoung/.

Young, S. and Caisey, V. (2015), 'Behavioral Economics and Social Marketing: Points of Contact?', Chapter 4 in: Stewart, D. (ed.), *Handbook of Persuasion and Social Marketing*, Volume II, New York: Praeger, 67–117.

Suggested reading

Akerlof, G. A. and Shiller, R. J. (2009), *Animal Spirits: How Human Psychology Drives the Economy, and Why It Matters for Global Capitalism*, Princeton: Princeton University Press.

Ariely, D. (2008), *Predictably Irrational*, London: Harper Collins.

Behavioural Insights Team. Various publications and blog.

Camerer, C. and Loewenstein, G. (2004), 'Behavioural Economics: Past, Present and Future', in: Camerer, C. F., Loewenstein, G. and Rabin, M. (eds.), *Advances in Behavioural Economics*, Princeton: Princeton University Press, pp. 3–53.

Kahneman, D. (2011), *Thinking Fast and Slow*, London: Allen Lane.

Schwartz, B. (2004), *The Paradox of Choice: Why More Is Less*, New York: Harper Perennial.

Thaler, R. (1994), *The Winner's Curse: Paradoxes and Anomalies of Economic Life*, Princeton: Princeton University Press.

Thaler, R. (2015), *Misbehaving*, London: Allen Lane.

Thaler, R. and Sunstein, C. (2008), *Nudge: Improving Decisions About Health, Wealth, and Happiness*, London: Penguin.

7 Complexity economics

Alan Kirman

Introduction

Economics has, for well over a hundred years, wanted to be considered as a 'science'. In order to achieve this, inevitably one must reduce what is an extremely complicated reality into a simple 'model', through which we may have some chance of explaining what causes what.

Now think, for a moment, of Tokyo's central railway station at rush hour. Viewed from above, it looks like an ants' nest, with lines of individuals forming as the insects go purposefully about their business. How should one reduce this to a simple model? One approach is to take an individual and try to understand what he or she is doing and why. It would clearly be very difficult to model every single individual, so one could instead try to understand how a 'typical' or 'representative' individual chooses what to do. This is the approach that mainstream economics has taken and, as the discipline has developed, this 'representative' individual has been portrayed as being capable of more and more sophisticated and calculating behaviour.

But think of another approach. Instead of studying this one 'typical' individual, we could recognise that we are dealing with a *collection* – often a very large collection – of individuals whose behaviour is influenced by each other. How would one simplify that? The answer is given in what is called the 'complex systems' approach, which lies at the heart of Complexity Economics. The following simple description of this was given by Herbert Simon:

> Roughly, by a complex system I mean one made up of a large number of parts that interact in a nonsimple way. In such systems, the whole is more than the sum of the parts, not in an ultimate, metaphysical sense, but in the important pragmatic sense that, *given the properties of the parts and the laws of their interaction*, it is not a trivial matter to infer the properties of the whole.
>
> Simon (1962)[1] pp. 467–468

The point is that one should not reduce the behaviour of the whole economy to that of a single sophisticated, calculating individual who works out what is good for himself in isolation. Rather, it is more realistic to think of the individuals as themselves being rather simple and as following basic 'rules of thumb'. It is then through their *interaction* with each other that a lot of interesting phenomena may emerge. How an ants' nest is structured and develops does not depend on any sort of sophisticated behaviour or organisation of individual ants, but rather upon the complexity of the interactions of the colony taken as a whole. In this way within human society too it makes little sense to explain how social phenomena, such as revolutions or stock market crashes, occur by studying individuals in isolation. Or, as Mervyn King, the former Governor of the Bank of England said:

> We should avoid the hubris of thinking that we understand how the economy works, just as we should avoid the hubris of thinking that leaving markets to their own devices will lead to nirvana.
>
> Mervyn King (April 2013)

In this chapter I will then contrast two simple alternatives when approaching the study of how economies function: the 'standard' approach adopted within mainstream economics, in which the economy is pictured as behaving like a single, very sophisticated individual; and the 'complex systems' approach, in which individuals are thought of as interacting with each other on the basis of simple rules, in such a way so as to produce often complicated aggregate behaviour, not directly deducible from individual behaviour taken in isolation.

In this chapter I will look briefly at some of the problems with the standard approach and will argue that the complexity vision offers a more realistic and useful alternative.

Equilibrium

One of the key differences between these two approaches is in the importance attributed to 'equilibrium'. Think of an economy in which every consumer knows the prices of all the goods available, now and in the future, and also knows what their income is and will be. Given this information they decide what goods they want to buy with the only constraint that what they want to buy should not cost more, in total, than their income. Firms, knowing the prices of goods and the level of wages, decide how much of each good to produce. Now the question is, will all of these choices be consistent? If the prices of the goods and the wages are such that the total amount of each good produced by all the firms is just equal to the total amount of each good chosen by all the consumers, then we say that the aggregate supply of each good is equal to the aggregate demand for each good and that the economy is in equilibrium.

The analysis of such equilibrium states is a defining preoccupation of the standard approach. This is partly because, as summarised in the 'First Fundamental Theorem of Welfare Economics', a perfectly competitive economy in equilibrium, as described above, is said to be 'efficient' in that no individual can be made better off without making someone else worse off. However, one of the first questions that may occur to an economics student is, how does the economy get to such an equilibrium? Depending on the particular stage in his or her studies, the answer may vary. Initially, he or she will be told that Adam Smith's 'invisible hand' somewhat mysteriously achieves this equilibrium. If individuals are left to their own devices, the economy will reach an equilibrium, which will have the socially desirable property of efficiency. How this will happen, however, is not made clear. Phrases such as 'markets do the job' are invoked. In weak moments even some very distinguished economists have claimed that we are able to *prove* that a 'perfectly competitive' economy will attain an equilibrium. The task is thus to study these equilibria and how they might change over time.

No such proof, however, has ever actually been forthcoming. One adjustment mechanism often invoked in this context, known as the "tatonnement" process, was first discussed by Léon Walras (1877). This refers to the lowering of prices of goods where firms are producing more than people want to buy and the raising of prices of those goods where consumers want to buy more than firms are producing. The alert student will immediately have two questions about this. Firstly, why should the price of the same good be identical across a market? Casual observation shows that this is not the case. Their second question would be, *who* adjusts all these prices to bring the market into equilibrium? Suspend your disbelief for a moment and imagine that there was some such figure. What three famous mathematical economists – Hugo Sonnenschein (1972), Rolf Mantel (1974) and Gérard Debreu (1974) – showed was highly destructive. They proved that, even with all the unrealistic assumptions about the behaviour of the individual economic agents and the economy being 'perfectly competitive', the tatonnement process would not necessarily lead the economy to an equilibrium. At this point many economic theorists suggested that it would be enough to propose another adjustment process. However, it rapidly became clear that this would not solve the problem. The adjustment processes suggested simply used too much information, and Saari and Simon (1978) put the final nail in the coffin by showing that an adjustment mechanism which would take an economy from any initial set of non-equilibrium prices to an equilibrium would necessarily require an infinite amount of information.

But all of this turned on the basic idea that what should interest us are the equilibria of an economy. According to the complexity approach, if we are really interested in explaining and understanding economic phenomena, then we should not confine ourselves to simply looking at equilibria and their properties. The complexity approach takes seriously the idea of an economic system that is constantly organising itself and that never settles down to an equilibrium. In so doing, it aims to address one of the central failings of standard economic theory. Indeed, it has long been recognised by policy makers that when a crisis arises, standard theory has remarkably little to say. One could cite governors of central banks, chief economists of the World Bank and other international organisations, all of whom explain that conventional analysis did not help them in the recent crisis. Why is that? Simply because if you study economies which are 'in equilibrium' you rule out, by assumption, major crises in which very clearly some markets, such as the labour market, are not in equilibrium.

Alternative approaches

In the face of such problems, different economists reacted in different ways. Some decided that we should simply stick with the basic model, modifying the assumptions a little to make it fit the data better. This is far from being a new phenomenon. Indeed, just as the Ptolomeans resisted the arguments of Copernicus, so many economists continue to adhere to their models, trying in vain to 'calibrate' them so as to make them fit the facts.

Others, instead, suggested a radical departure from standard models that base themselves on equilibrium analysis and strong assumptions about individual optimisation. Werner Hildenbrand (1994), one of the leading General Equilibrium theorists, even went so far as to say that we should completely abandon the assumptions we make about the principal actor in our economic play, 'homo economicus', and his extreme rationality and just look at the empirical distribution of the choices actually made by individuals in real life. This call to base our theory on the empirical evidence, an approach which is so integral to the physical sciences, fell, unfortunately, on deaf ears.

The Complex Systems approach has emerged in response to this call and is now regularly being discussed not only in academic circles but also in central banks such as the Bank of England, in international organisations such as the Organisation for Economic Co-operation and Development (OECD) and in a number of finance ministries such as the U.S. Treasury.

Comparing the standard and the complex system approaches

The standard approach

As described above, the standard approach to economics focuses upon the characterisation of equilibria within markets. Economies are thought of as jumping from one equilibrium to another in response to 'exogenous' shocks, that is to say to changes in the environment that are entirely external to the decision making of the individuals within an economy, such as an unexpected technological advance or change in government policy.

A major requirement of such standard models of the economy is that they be built on 'sound microfoundations'. By this it is meant that the models are built around individuals who, in isolation, and given the constraints with which they are faced – typically budget constraints for consumers and technical constraints on production for firms – attempt to 'optimise', that is, to achieve the best possible alternative available to them. What is meant by 'best', for the consumers, is in terms of what they prefer.

Typically, standard theory imposes stringent conditions on how people's preferences are understood in order to ensure that their choices are 'rational'. Preferences are, for instance, modelled as always being coherent. This means that if in one instance a person chooses an alternative A over another alternative B when both were available to them, they should *never* choose B over A when both are possible. Such inconsistency would be 'irrational', and as such, we should not expect to observe this in reality. This perhaps sounds reasonable at first, but once one thinks a bit more carefully, this is a very strong assumption. People frequently change their choices from one day to the next, for no reason other than that they fancied the change. Mainstream economic theorists often respond to this problem by arguing that there is, in fact, no contradiction here: the fish that the consumer preferred to bananas last week is not the same good as the fish that they now reject for bananas this week. 'Fish *this week*' is a good all of its own. However, whilst such subtlety resolves the apparent 'contradictions' observable in everyday behaviour, it in turn makes the 'consistency' assumption described above entirely unverifiable, since two choices are *always* made at different points in time. This and other assumptions that are made about peoples' preferences have been the subject of over a century of debate. Indeed, Vilfredo Pareto, who is often considered with Walras to be the father of modern mathematical economics, when he turned to sociology, remarked that he felt that individuals spent some of their time making non-rational decisions and the rest of their time rationalising them. The truth is that our assumptions about the rationality of people's behaviour have been based on introspection and not on the actual observed behaviour of individuals.

As soon as we start to worry about how people take their uncertain future into account, we also have to worry about how they forecast their future environment. If people can have any expectations whatsoever about the future, then we cannot say very much at all. Typically in the standard approach, the simplifying assumption is made that people not only have the same expectations but that these expectations are consistent with the way the economy actually evolves (the so-called rational expectations hypothesis, discussed further below). You will, of course, wonder how individuals come to form such expectations, and a number of economists have indeed struggled with that problem.

The preoccupation with 'microfoundations' typical of the standard approach is also witnessed in the tendency to look only to individual characteristics. In other words, we should not worry about how agents interact directly with each other or about the structure of that interaction. Within this view, social networks, for example, do not have a role in determining aggregate economic outcomes.

Such simplifications make life easy for economic theorists, but the assumptions about the world needed to make them credible are so restrictive that they are often not all that helpful when analysing the evolution of real economies.

Furthermore, there is a focus on efficient outcomes within the standard approach, and thereby neglects the major problem of economics of explaining how so many disparate individuals manage to coordinate their different activities. For many students the unreasonableness of these assumptions made in standard economic analysis and the heavy investment required in specific mathematical tools is enough to make them abandon the subject early on. But it is possible to think of the economy differently and no less rigorously.

The complex systems approach

According to this view, individuals within an economy follow simple rules of thumb to determine their course of action. However, they adapt to their environment by changing the rules they use when these prove to be less successful. They are not irrational in that they do not act against their own interests, but they have neither the information nor the calculating capacity to 'optimise'. Indeed, they are assumed to have limited and largely local information, and they modify their behaviour to improve their situation. Individuals in complexity models are neither assumed to understand how the economy works nor to consciously look for the 'best choice'. The main preoccupation is not whether aggregate outcomes are efficient or not but rather with how all of these different individuals interacting with each other come to coordinate their behaviour.

Giving individuals in a model simple rules to follow and allowing them to change them as they interact with others means thinking of them much more like particles or social insects. Mainstream economists often object to this approach, arguing that humans have intentions and aims which cannot be found in either inanimate particles or lower forms of life. However, this argument is not fully convincing. Within the standard approach, individuals' intentions are modelled in terms of their preferences and expectations. Once we have endowed our representative agent with a certain set of preferences and a rule for forecasting what will happen in the future, he is very much like an automaton who will mechanically respond to what is going on.

The important thing about considering the economy as a complex system is that one can then deal with heterogeneous agents and, in particular, ones whose characteristics may change as the behaviour of those around them changes. Within a complexity model, individuals interact with, influence and are influenced by those around them. Behaviour in the aggregate emerges from this interaction as individuals adapt to the situation around them but, crucially, it cannot be predicted by looking at any single individual.

Within a complex systems approach, systems can, as they evolve, go through major changes without requiring any 'exogenous', outside shock. This principle is demonstrated well by John Conway's "Game of Life", a computer simulation game. It is a famous early example of how a system, in which the individuals respect very simple rules, may have a constantly changing aggregate configuration or may settle to a fixed pattern. The game consists of a grid of cells, much like that of a giant chess board, each of which are either 'alive' or 'dead'. They continue to live, die or are born depending on the states of their neighbours. Many animated illustrations of the "Game of Life" may be found on the Web.

In much the same way as in this simple toy model, consider a market in which the participants decide to buy, hold or sell a stock by following what the majority of those with whom they are linked (their neighbours) do. Add a few extra conditions, for example, as to how prices evolve depending on how much of the stock is demanded or supplied, let the individuals make some mistakes from time to time, and the market will develop large fluctuations which are not caused by any 'outside' influence but just by individuals deciding what to do as a function of what their neighbours are doing. In this example, as in the "Game of Life", you have the ingredients of a complex system. The participants act as a function of the state they are in (in this case, how much stock they hold), and their choices evolve depending on what their neighbours choose to do. This sort of picture seems a much more appropriate view of how markets evolve rather than one in which the system settles to an equilibrium position and then gets knocked out of that equilibrium by some external shock.

An example: racial segregation

To illustrate these points, let's look at an important social problem, that of racial segregation. Racial segregation is a persistent phenomenon in many cities in many countries. In the US, for example, while more than one-half of Black Americans now live in middle- or upper-income households, segregation in housing has persisted in major cities. The natural explanation for this phenomena would be that individuals are racist and prefer to avoid living with people of another race. Thus, segregation is no more than a macro-phenomenon that reflects, in a consistent way, people's individual sentiments. But Tom Schelling, the 2005 Nobel Prize winner in economics whose influence permeates much of what we now call complex economics, showed, once again, that the relationship between micro- and macro-behaviour is not so simple. He argued that the degree of segregation which we observe is far from reflecting individual views. At the end of the 1960s, he introduced a model of segregation (a good summary of the variants of his model is given in Schelling (1978)), which showed essentially that even if people have only a very mild preference for living with neighbours of their own colour, as they move to satisfy their preferences, complete segregation can occur.

To see what is at work here, it is worth looking in some detail at the model that Schelling introduced. It can be explained simply and intuitively, and this is one of the features of Schelling's contributions that makes them so appealing and which generated such surprise. A fuller account of this surprising relationship between micro-features and aggregate phenomena in the segregation model or, to use Schelling's original phrase, the relationship between 'micromotives and macrobehavior', can be found in the paper by Pancs and Vriend (2007).

The basic idea is this: take a large chess board and place a certain number of dark and light counters on the board, leaving some free spaces. The basic assumption is that each counter prefers to be on a square where, at most, four of his eight neighbours are of a different colour than his own. As long as fewer than half of their neighbours are of a different colour from their own, the individual is happy, or has high utility, as mainstream economists might say. However, if the number of different-coloured neighbours passes this threshold, then the individual becomes unhappy.

At each step an individual is drawn at random, and if they are unhappy, that is, have low utility, they move to the nearest unoccupied space where their utility will be higher. An example of what happens over 'time' (i.e. over the course of many individual steps) is illustrated in Figure 7.1, which shows segregation developing rapidly.

Indeed, Schelling showed that the result would, in general, be complete segregation. This is, in some sense, rather surprising in that the segregated outcome does not reflect the relative tolerance of the individuals. However, as Vinkovic and Kirman (2006) point out, a physicist would not be so surprised: oil and water do not naturally tend to mix, and such a mixture rapidly sorts out into two separate layers. They develop a simple physical analogy to the Schelling puzzle, which shows clearly what is going on. It is sometimes useful for economists to cast a glance at other disciplines!

The results above resulted from just one of the many possible 'utility functions' that we might use to determine how individuals behave in this environment. Perhaps more surprising is what happens when all individuals instead prefer perfectly balanced neighbourhoods, such that their utility is only high when *exactly* half of their neighbours share their own colour. The result of conducting the same experiment with individuals of this type is illustrated in the lower panels of Figure 7.2.

The result can be compared to the outcome of the original utility function, shown in the upper panels. The situation in the lower panels looks remarkably similar: almost total segregation. Nevertheless, at the micro level, the situations could not be more different. With the original utility function, there is almost no movement after a certain point in

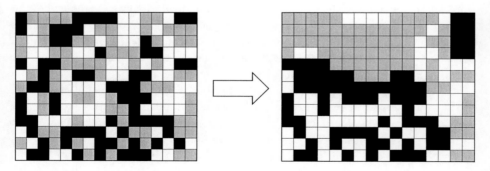

Figure 7.1 Segregation emerging from 'non–discriminatory' preferences
Source: Pancs and Vriend (2007)

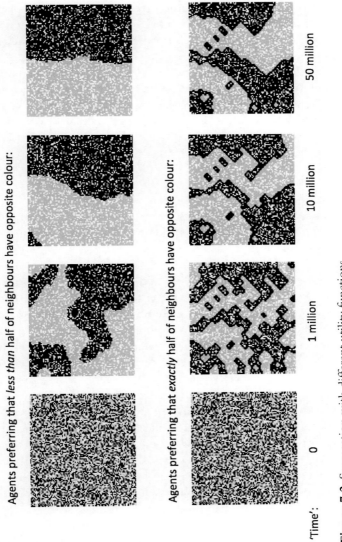

Figure 7.2 Segregation with different utility functions

Source: Pancs and Vriend (2007)

time. The great majority of the individuals are happy and have no incentive to move. Yet with the new utility function, the individuals in the population are constantly moving. From a distance the situation looks like a static one comparable to the original experiment, but in the second experiment, almost nobody is happy and people are constantly looking for a better square. The reason for this is obvious: an exact balance of neighbours between the two colours is easily disturbed. As soon as one person moves, the fine balance is destroyed, thereby creating an incentive to move for all former neighbours. Thus, the similarity between the two models is illusory, because macro similarity is not equivalent to micro similarity.

Many of the key lessons of Complexity Economics can be learnt from analysing this very simple model and its variations. We see that systems of interacting particles or 'agents' can have a tendency to self-organize, the results of which may be very different from what one might have anticipated and may not be socially satisfactory from the aggregate point of view.

Markets

The idea that markets have an intrinsic stability is a central myth born of the standard approach to economics. As Adair Turner, previously the head of the Financial Services Authority in the UK, said:

> But there is also a strong belief, which I share, that bad or rather over-simplistic and overconfident economics helped create the crisis. There was a dominant conventional wisdom that markets were always rational and self-equilibrating, that market completion by itself could ensure economic efficiency and stability, and that financial innovation and increased trading activity were therefore axiomatically beneficial.
> *Adair Turner, Head of the U.K. Financial Services Authority. Speech at the*
> *City Banquet, Mansion House, London, 22 September 2009*

The idea that markets, left to their own devices, are self-stabilising has been used as a justification for deregulating financial markets and for removing as many controls on banks' activities as possible. The basic rationale behind this is what is called the "efficient market" hypothesis, which was originally developed by Bachelier in 1900. His argument was simple. Each individual, independently, receives some private information, which he or she then acts upon. The result of the act is to reveal his or her private information to all others. In this way all available information is transmitted through asset prices. Therefore, nobody needs to look at anything but the current market prices.

There are two problems with this. Firstly, as Grossman and Stiglitz (1980) pointed out long ago, if there were really no need to look at anything but market prices, nobody would look at their private information which, as a result, would never be incorporated into prices. Secondly, it ignores the possibility of 'herd' behaviour. As

Poincaré, the famous 19th–20th-century mathematician (and referee for Bachelier's thesis) later said:

> When people are in close contact with each other they no longer decide randomly and independently of each other. Many factors come into play, and they disturb people, shifting them one way and then the other, but there is one thing that they will not destroy and that is people's tendency to behave like sheep. It is that which will always persist.
>
> Henri Poincaré (1908), *Science et Methode*, p. 49 (author's translation)

For Poincaré, this natural tendency to herd undermined Bachelier's theory. Nonetheless, the Efficient Markets Hypothesis which developed out of his theory has become the basis, not only for modern financial theory but for much of the policies for regulating – or not regulating – such markets.

To see how herding, which undermines the theory, can occur, suppose that the system is such that when agents expect higher prices, prices do, in fact, turn out to be higher. This is what is referred to as positive feedback, or, to use George Soros' term, "reflexivity". This sort of self-reinforcement is like the behaviour of ants who herd on one food source: each time an ant follows the trail to that source, it lays more phero-mone, thereby attracting more ants. But, notice that there is nothing unreasonable or 'irrational' about such herd behaviour, unless we adopt the narrow definition of that term often used in standard economics.

How can this sort of behaviour be seen in financial markets? There is a long and well-documented history of financial bubbles, including the tulip bubble, the South Sea bubble and much more recently the 'dotcom' bubble, the housing bubbles in the U.S., the derivatives bubbles and very recently the Bitcoin bubble. Using the ideas suggested by the behaviour of ants, it is easy to build models which generate bubbles as individuals focus on one forecasting rule and then another (see Föllmer et al. [2005]), just as ants switch from one food source to another. The sort of interactions and positive feedbacks involved are typical of complex systems but are largely absent in standard macroeconomic models. The key features of such models are (1) that aggregate behaviour emerges from the interaction between the individuals and cannot be predicted from just looking at the individuals in isolation; (2) that these systems self-organise but may never settle to an 'equilibrium' as they are constantly evolving; (3) the individuals in the system may have rather simple behaviour, and again the interaction between the individuals generates the complex behaviour of the whole; and (4) this direct interaction between individuals is a central and defining feature and not just some sort of friction.

To get an idea as to how these ideas can help us understand the Global Financial Cri-sis, for example, it is worth looking at a key part of the system. In the Mortgage Backed Securities (MBS) market, a puzzle was that prices did not gradually go down as the housing market worsened and as more and more mortgages became delinquent. Why were indi-viduals and banks buying these instruments in these circumstances and why was their price not falling? A simple explanation is that it is costly to check on the mortgages underlying the assets, and if the participants in the market observe that those around them are not checking, then they may buy themselves, knowing that, with a high probability, they can sell the instrument without the purchaser checking. However, this situation is fragile. As the knowledge that many of the derivatives are toxic spreads, then finally some participants will check. Seeing this happen, however, others will also start to check, and the market will collapse as the toxicity of the assets becomes apparent. This seems to be a reasonable explanation, at least in part, for the collapse of the MBS market. But such a collapse was not triggered by some major external shock – the downturn in house prices, for instance, happened some time before the collapse of the MBS market – but rather was due to a combination of contagion in the network of buyers together with changing perceptions of the situation. This is far from the view of the world in standard economics in which all actors are well aware of the real situation and in which they take fully informed rational decisions. Here there is something more like an epidemic of doubt.[2] Again, we see that small shocks at the individual level may translate into major crises at the aggregate level.

Expectations

In an economy where there is uncertainty about the future, the expectations that individuals have play an important role. If macroeconomics is to be able to define an equilibrium, it has to be one into which expectations enter. Clearly, in an uncertain world, what people or firms supply and demand will be based on current prices but also on their anticipation of future prices. But, if individuals may have any expectations whatsoever about future prices, it is not clear at what current prices there will be an equilibrium. One way out of this, adopted in the standard approach to economics, is to assume that all the participants in an economy fully understand its functioning and evolution. They therefore have the same anticipations, too. Such anticipations are referred to as 'Rational Expectations'.

Bearing in mind the quote from Mervyn King given at the outset of this chapter, this seems an heroic assumption. Furthermore, there is a great deal of evidence that people do not have the same expectations. Worse, their expectations are not independent but are, rather, strongly influenced by the expectations of others, exactly as Poincaré suggested. As such, they cannot be treated as being randomly distributed around an 'average' point of view. As Willem Buiter, the chief economist of Citibank, observed:

> Those of us who worry about endogenous uncertainty arising from the interactions of boundedly rational market participants cannot but scratch our heads at the insistence of the mainline models that all uncertainty is exogenous and additive.
>
> Buiter (2009)

Many economists have expressed doubt about the notion of rational expectations which is, in reality, just a convenient way of making standard models tractable. We have no explanation as to just why agents should come to have such expectations. As such, a more pragmatic approach would be to go back to the basics and study how, in fact, economic actors do form their expectations. As Herbert Simon said,

> A very natural next step for economics is to maintain expectations in the strategic position they have come to occupy, but to build an empirically validated theory of how attention is in fact directed within a social system, and how expectations are, in fact, formed. Taking that next step requires that empirical work in economics take a new direction, the direction of micro-level investigation proposed by Behavioralism.
>
> Simon (1984)

Such a step would undoubtedly mark a major change for economics. Some progress has been made in this direction through laboratory experiments, and there is already considerable evidence that individuals, even though perfectly informed about the income generated by an asset in the future, can still generate bubbles in the asset's price, thereby contradicting the rational expectations hypothesis. Again, what we see is the interaction between the individuals who observe the actions taken by others, which can generate a positive feedback. It is these features, characteristic of complex systems, which generate such bubbles.[3]

Conclusion

Overall, it would perhaps be wise to listen to the pragmatic and realistic point of view put forward by former chairman of the U.S. Federal Reserve, Ben Bernanke:

> I just think it is not realistic to think that human beings can fully anticipate all possible interactions and complex developments. The best approach for dealing with this uncertainty is to make sure that the system is fundamentally resilient and that we have as many fail-safes and back-up arrangements as possible.
>
> Ben Bernanke, Interview with the *International Herald Tribune*, May 17, 2010

Notice that this is an admission that, in the context of a deregulated financial sector, no invisible hand or self-organisation of the agents in the system will necessarily lead it to a socially satisfactory solution. In fact, policy makers in Central Banks and organisations such as the International Monetary Fund (IMF) and the OECD, have come to accept that the economic system is in need of constant monitoring and corrective measures. Given the complexity of the system, and the complication of dealing with people with different expectations, this is inevitable.

In this brief chapter I have argued that the vision of the economy conveyed by standard models, particularly macroeconomic models, does not give an adequate account of how the economic system evolves. The vision of the economy as a system which self-organises into a socially satisfactory state is the outcome of two centuries of the philosophical development of a social and political tendency toward liberalism. Economics has developed its theory so as to derive a model which is consistent with that philosophical position. Yet, as our models have become more and more mathematically sophisticated, they have tended to become more and more remote from the reality of the economic world in which we live.

Reconsidering our basic framework and viewing the economy as a complex adaptive system in which macro-behaviour emerges from the interaction between the participants in the economy would help us in a number of ways. Firstly, in such a model endogenous shocks can occur, and crises do not have to be attributed to what Adam Smith referred to as "The Invisible Hand of Jupiter". Secondly, we do not have to attribute to individuals the remarkable capacity to calculate and acquire a complete knowledge of how the economy functions that the 'representative individual' in standard models is assumed to have. Lastly, we do not have to suggest that there are simple mechanical relations between actions taken and economic outcomes. In complex systems there is always the possibility of 'unintended consequences'. Rather than claim that we know what the result of policy measures will be, a complex systems approach proposes a paradigm which makes much less authoritative claims, and requires those in charge of making economic policy to anticipate and try to moderate the evolution of the economy without being able to make precise predictions. Despite Walras's claim that one day its laws would be as irrefutable as those of astrophysics, economics is not and never will be an 'exact science' in the sense that is too often claimed for it.

Notes

1 H. A. Simon, 'The Architecture of Complexity', *Proceedings of the American Philosophical Society*, vol. 106, iss. 6, pp. 467–482, 1962.
2 For an account and a model of this sort of phenomenon, see e.g Anand et al. (2013).
3 A very good account of such experiments is given in Cars Hommes (2013).

References

Anand, K., Kirman, A. and Marsili M. (2013), 'Epidemics of rules, rational negligence and market crashes', *The European Journal of Finance*, Vol. 19, No. 5, pp. 438–447.
Basu, K. (2010), *Beyond the Invisible Hand: Groundwork for a New Economics*, Princeton: Princeton University Press.
Buiter, W. (2009), 'The Unfortunate Uselessness of Most "State of the Art" Academic Monetary Economics', retrieved from: http://blogs.ft.com/maverecon/2009/03/the-unfortunate-uselessness-of-most-state-of-the-art-academic-monetary-economics/#axzz4oLRtLrtv.
Debreu, G. (1974), 'Excess Demand Functions', *Journal of Mathematical Economics*, Vol. 1, No. 1, pp. 15–23.

Föllmer, H., Horst, U. and Kirman, A. (2005), 'Equilibria in Financial Markets With Heterogeneous Agents: A Probabilistic Perspective', *Journal of Mathematical Economics*, Vol. 41, No. 1–2, pp. 123–155.

Grossman, S. J. and Stiglitz, J. E. (1980), 'On the Impossibility of Informationally Efficient Markets', *American Economic Review*, Vol. 70, No. 3, pp. 393–408.

Hildenbrand, W. (1994), *Market Demand: Theory and Empirical Evidence*, Princeton, NJ: Princeton University Press.

Hommes, C. (2013), *Behavioral Rationality and Heterogeneous Expectations in Complex Economic Systems*, Cambridge: Cambridge University Press.

Kartik, A., Kirman, A. and Marsili, M. (2013), 'Epidemics of Rules, Rational Negligence and Market Crashes', *European Journal of Finance*, Vol. 19, No. 5, pp. 438–447.

Lucas, R. E. Jr. (2003), 'Macroeconomic Priorities', *American Economic Review*, Vol. 93, No. 1, pp. 1–14.

Mantel, R. (1974), 'On the Characterisation of Aggregate Excess Demand', *Journal of Economic Theory*, Vol. 7, pp. 348–353.

Mas-Colell, A., Whinston, M. D. and Green, J. R. (1995), *Microeconomic Theory*, New York, Oxford: Oxford University Press.

Pancs, R. and Vriend, N. J. (2007), 'Schelling's Spatial Proximity Model of Segregation Revisited', *Journal of Public Economics*, Vol. 91, pp. 1–24.

Poincaré, H. (1908), *Science et Methode*, Paris: Flammarion.

Rodrik, D. (2015), *Economics Rules: The Rights and Wrongs of the Dismal Science*, New York: W. W. Norton & Co.

Romer, P. (2016), 'The Trouble With Macroeconomics', *The American Economist*, forthcoming.

Saari, D. and Simon, C. P. (1978), 'Effective Price Mechanisms', *Econometrica*, Vol. 46, pp. 1097–1125.

Schelling, T. S. (1978), *Micromotives and Macrobehavior*, New York: W.W. Norton & Co.

Simon, H. (1984), 'On the Behavioral and Rational Foundations of Economic Dynamics', *Journal of Economic Behavior and Organisation*, Vol. 5, No. 1, pp. 35–55.

Simon, H. (1962), 'The Architecture of Complexity', *Proceedings of the American Philosophical Society*, Vol. 106, No. 6, pp. 467–482.

Smith, A. (1776), *An Inquiry into the Nature and Causes of the Wealth of Nations*, London: Methuen & Co.

Sonnenschein, H. (1972), 'Market Excess Demand Functions', *Econometrica*, Vol. 40, pp. 549–563.

Trichet, J.-C. (2010), Opening Address at the ECB Central Banking Conference, Frankfurt, 18 November, retrieved from: www.ecb.europa.eu/press/key/date/2010/html/sp101118.en.html.

Vinkovic, D. and Kirman, A. (2006), 'A Physical Analogue of the Schelling Model', *Proceedings of the National Academy of Sciences*, Vol. 103, pp. 19261–19265.

Walras, L. (1877), *Elements d'economie politique pure ou Theorie de la Richesse Sociale*, First Edition, Lausanne: L. Corbaz.

Suggested further readings

Arthur, W. B. (2015), *Complexity and the Economy*, Oxford: Oxford University Press.

Kirman, A. (2011), *Complex Economics: Individual and Collective Rationality*, London: Routledge.

For books which adopt similar approaches, start with the classic:
Schelling, T. S. (1978), *Micromotives and Macrobehavior*, New York: W. W. Norton & Co.

Other references, particularly for agent–based modelling:
Caiani, A., Russo, A., Palestrini, A. and Gallegati, M. (2016), *Economies With Heterogeneous Interacting Agents: A Practical Guide to Agent Based Modelling*, New York: Springer Verlag.
Epstein, J. M. (2007), *Generative Social Science: Studies in Agent-Based Computational Modeling*, Princeton, NJ: Princeton University Press.
Epstein, J. M. (2014), *Agent Zero: Toward Neurocognitive Foundations for Generative Social Science*, Princeton Studies in Complexity, Princeton, NJ: Princeton University Press.
Miller, J. and Page, S. (2007), *Complex Adaptive Systems: An Introduction to Computational Models of Social Life*, Princeton and Oxford: Princeton University Press.

A collection of earlier articles in:
Arthur, W. B., Durlauf, S. N. and Lane, D. (eds.) (1997), *The Economy as an Evolving Complex System II*, Redwood City, CA: Addison Wesley.

Just in case you might think that the crisis is new:
Reinhart, C. M. and Rogoff, K. S. (2010), *This Time Is Different: A Panoramic View of Eight Centuries of Financial Crises*, Princeton, NJ: Princeton University Press.

A reaction of policy makers:
Turner, A. (2013), *Economics After the Crisis: Objectives and Means*, Cambridge, MA: MIT Press.

A sociological approach:
Granovetter, J. (1997), *Society and Economy: The Social Construction of Economic Institutions*, Cambridge, MA: Harvard University Press.

Lessons from social insects:
Gordon, D. (2010), *Ant Encounters: Interaction Networks and Colony Behavior*, Princeton: Princeton University Press.
Seeley, T. (2012), *Honeybee Democracy*, Princeton: Princeton University Press.

8 Co-operative economics

Molly Scott Cato

Introduction

Neoclassical economics is a school of economic thought that is dedicated to analysing capitalism – a fact that is reflected in its theoretical assumptions. Since co-operatives represent an alternative form of economic organisation to capitalism, they require an alternative economic theory. The classic division between supply and demand dissolves in an organisation where producers and consumers co-operate over production standards, price and quantity. Nor are co-operatives driven by classic capitalist motivations such as profit and growth. For a co-operative, profits are surpluses, and deriving them needs to be balanced against fair terms and conditions for employees and suppliers.[1] Growth is desirable only up to a certain size, at which point the requirement for engagement and shared decision making is made more difficult by the sheer number of people involved.

In this chapter I address some key economic questions. However, instead of making assumptions tailored to the capitalist system, I will work from the understanding that resources should be fairly shared and the needs of producers and consumers balanced rather than in competition. This leads us to some quite distinct ideas about the optimal structure of markets and economic organisations.

So what is a co-operative? According to the International Co-operative Alliance, "a co-operative is an autonomous association of persons united voluntarily to meet their common economic, social, and cultural needs and aspirations through a jointly-owned and democratically-controlled enterprise." The word 'autonomous' is important since it requires that membership is voluntary and workers or customers cannot be required to join a co-operative in order to work or shop there. The nature of democratic control of the enterprise differs from co-operative to co-operative depending on size and sector, but it does not conform to the traditional, hierarchical management structure of a capitalist enterprise.

Co-operatives are often established when people discover that the capitalist economy is not meeting their needs. For example, somebody might need housing and discover that if they join with other people in the same situation, they can improve their ability to buy property, thus creating a housing co-operative. In a similar way, the co-operatives that still dominate the market for whole foods in the UK were a response by individual consumers who found they could not buy the natural, organic food they wanted to eat. The co-operative movement actually began in the food sector, with working people creating their own supply networks to avoid being exploited by monopolistic shops.

The definition also stresses the importance of working together to solve problems. As Co-operatives UK explains: "What makes co-operatives unique is that they are run not by institutional investors or distant shareholders, but by their members. People like you and me – customers, employees, residents, farmers, artists, taxi drivers". This sharing impulse explains why in some sectors, particularly the financial and health sectors, co-operatives are sometimes referred to as 'mutuals'. The mutual ethic also helps explain the different and more equal relationship between producers and consumers that typifies co-operative businesses. Producers and consumers can cut out the middle man, ensuring lower prices for consumers and higher returns for producers. As we will see later, this was a central motive for the original foundation of co-operatives.

This is not a mere theoretical discussion. Across the world today, millions of people are members or employees of co-operatives. Across many different sectors such as agriculture, housing, finance or retail, there are co-operatives operating successfully as an alternative to the private business model. This means that it is possible to organise almost every aspect of your life under the co-operative aegis. Co-operatives are found in every corner of the world and are among the biggest businesses: for example, the Zen-Noh, the National Association of Agricultural Co-operatives in Japan, had an annual turnover of $57 billion in 2012, more or less matching the turnover of the French co-operative supermarket Leclerc.

The chapter begins with a brief introduction to the theory and history of co-operative economic activity. It moves on to question the basic assumption of a capitalist economy: namely, that resources are owned by private interests and that most people must make a living in the absence of resources and through their own work. The next section explores how a system of production and distribution might work if we looked at society as a whole and considered all its members as playing a role on both the production and consumption sides of the economy. The following section considers the issue of exchange of goods between companies and nations and how this might be conceptualised from within a co-operative paradigm. Finally, I explore how a co-operative economy might have an impact on wider society, and the spillover effects that might arise if economic organisations operated according to co-operative principles.

Theory and history of cooperation in brief

The impulse for the growth of the co-operative movement arose from a critique of capitalist production which suggested that while the real value in productive enterprise was created by workers, a significant amount of it was extracted by owners who had only invested their capital but not expended any labour. The idea of the co-operative is to remove such external owners so that the employees themselves own the firm, control their own work and any surplus generated will either be reinvested in the firm or paid to employees as bonuses.

Many of the earlier co-operators, including Robert Owen, who is considered to be the father of the movement, were proponents of what is known as the 'labour theory of value'. This holds that the relative value of commodities traded in a market is determined by the amount of labour required to produce them (Marxist economists also subscribe to this theory: see Chapter 2). Owen had been a manager in a capitalist business and had observed how workers were paid the minimum to keep them alive and fit for work while the products of their labour were sold for much more than the cost of production, the resulting 'surplus value' accruing to the owner in the form of profit. He considered this an injustice and established a National Equitable Labour Exchange, where goods were exchanged according to the amount of time they required to be produced and using time-based money (Bickle and Cato, 2008). This was his first experiment with what he considered a system of exchange based on justice. He later proposed that workers should control their own labor and own the productive resources themselves, the key principle underpinning the co-operative movement.

While the theory of cooperation began on the production side, the practice was more focused on the consumption side of the market economy. The official history of the co-operative movement begins in Rochdale, England, with the Rochdale Pioneers and the establishment of their co-operative shop in 1844. They began trading household dry goods such as flour, oatmeal and sugar, which they bought from local suppliers. However, once the shop began to flourish, the co-operators cut out the middlemen to be able to reduce prices for their members as well as ensuring the food was pure and produced without exploitation (Shaw, 2008). An iconic product for the Co-operative Wholesale Society (which later came to form part of the UK consumer co-operative today known simply as 'The Co-operative') was tea, which it had sold to its enthusiastic members from the 1860s. In 1902 the Co-operative Tea Society bought estates in Sri Lanka to access its own supplies, and tea became a test of the movement's commitment to fair trading principles. In 1973 a document exposed exploitation on the tea plantations in Sri Lanka, including those owned by The Co-operative. After a process of soul searching about the extent of the co-operative's commitment to equity and fair trading, the UK co-operative movement's commitment to the development of fair trade for global products developed (Anderson, 2008).

There are a wide range of co-operatives that have aimed to balance the needs of producers and consumers in different ways, and three main types are recognised:

1   In *worker co-operatives*, those employed to work in the business also own that business; these are sometimes also referred to as primary co-operatives because they produce and sell a primary good or service. There are many examples of such co-operatives, including the famous Mondragon co-operative in the Basque country of Spain and Calvert Press, a London-based print company.

2 In *producer co-operatives*, groups of producers join together to retail their product; these are also known as secondary co-operatives because the co-operative activity takes place at the stage of marketing rather than production. The largest global examples are in the agricultural sector, especially the vast number of dairy co-operatives, such as Arla or Fonterra in New Zealand, as well as doctors or creative workers who come together to share work and marketing expenses.

3 Finally, in *consumer or retail co-operatives*, the customers create the co-operative in order to increase their power as consumers either by forming purchasing clubs or through organisations to manage necessary services. In this category we have the many global examples of co-operative shops, including The Co-operative as well as the many housing co-operatives across the world.

As outlined in the previous section, co-operative activity is defined by a fixed but evolving system of principles and values[2]:

- *Voluntary and open membership*: anybody can join no matter how few resources they have, and nobody can be forced to join.
- *Democratic member control*: co-operatives are controlled by their members, who actively participate in setting their policies and making decisions.
- *Member economic participation*: a co-operative represents a collective economic enterprise, and every member must contribute something financially to demonstrate their commitment.
- *Cooperation amongst co-operatives*: co-operatives see themselves as part of a movement and thus commit to a principle of solidarity among each other to prioritise other co-operatives when they purchase goods and services.

The best-known co-operative businesses in the world are those that make up the Mondragon group in the Basque country. Their example highlights many aspects of the theory of co-operation, as well as the challenges co-operatives face in the global economy. The region suffered high unemployment until the local priest, José María Arizmendiarrieta, founded a technical school in the 1940s because of his conviction that knowledge was the key to economic success. In 1956 several of his students started the first producer co-operative, Fagor, which has grown to become a European leader in the production of domestic electrical goods. The Mondragon Group now consists of 67 industrial enterprises, eight involved in distribution, and fifteen which serve the group as a whole, primarily in the educational field. Eroski, the leading chain of hypermarkets in northern Spain and with outlets throughout the country, and Caja Laboral, the workers' bank, are also members of the Mondragon Group (see Novkovic and Webb, 2014).

A co-operative perspective on resources

As an economist committed to co-operative economics, I have found Karl Polanyi to be a great inspiration. Polanyi reexamined the way in which capitalism deals with the basic resources necessary for commodity production. In neoclassical economics these are defined as 'factors of production', and the three fundamental ones are land, labour and capital (Polanyi, 1944). Polanyi critiqued the attempt to commodify these basic building blocks of economic life via the creation of what he termed 'fictitious commodities'.[3] How could living, breathing people be reduced to 'labour', he asked, and how could the wealth of the natural world be limited to the narrow category of 'land'? Capital is perhaps the most fictitious of the three: an artificial means for those who own goods to maintain the power that ownership conveys through time and across distance. The radical potential in Polanyi's theory is that it raises the question of whether the ownership of such 'fictitious commodities' is defensible or even coherent. The capitalist economic system relies on a legally enforced system of private property rights, but these rights have no universal validity.

Polanyi's theoretical conclusions were based on extensive fieldwork, exploring how human communities across the world answered key economic questions. What he discovered was that in most societies economic life is a social process; the reduction of economic life to a series of market-based transactions is a recent phenomenon. We would do well to remember this when we analyse our own economy since it helps us understand that the movement away from meeting our own needs directly – a process sometimes referred to as 'self-provisioning' – and towards the marketisation of ever more areas of life is still on-going, for example with ready-made meals and universal childcare. In many societies people continue to provide for their own needs directly, as subsistence farmers. Examples are farmers working on the land released to people through land reform in the Philippines or on allotments like the *zahradky* ('little gardens') that are a feature of life in the Czech Republic that has survived the transition from Communism. Similar allotments were introduced in societies that were newly industrialised to allow those now working in factories to continue to grow crops and raise chickens and perhaps a pig.

Co-operative economics seeks to take a holistic perspective on the economy, to see us all as simultaneously producers and consumers, and to re-embed our economic life in wider social communities and natural environments. By contrast, the market approach to economics encourages us to seek low prices in our role as consumers, even though this might cause us to lose opportunities to act as producers because production is off-shored to countries with lower environmental standards and wages. In other words, it is a form of economic divide-and-rule. Co-operative economic theory questions who has a right to own the resources in an economy and then extends that question to ask how the increased value of the products made with those resources should be shared. In a market economy, profit is made by charging the highest prices that consumers can be pressured or cajoled into paying. This is justified by appeal to the 'laws' of supply and demand, but in fact both can be manipulated. For example, scarcity can be created intentionally to increase the price, and demand can be manufactured through advertising. Apple, as an example of a powerful oligopolistic corporation, uses both of these techniques to ensure that it can charge high prices for its latest models.

The key question driving a co-operative approach to economics is: who creates the value in the economy, and what does that imply about how that value should be shared?

So, in the case of a new computer or mobile phone, the fair price would be related to the cost of the materials used to manufacture it, including the wages paid to those who worked in the manufacturing plant. The maximisation of profit through production in low-wage economies and sale to over-excited consumers in distant wealthy markets, the very system that characterizes 21st-century capitalism, would be anathema to a co-operative economist. As we will see in the section on trade, the fair trade movement is a practical response to this ethical position.

A co-operative theory of the firm

So far, we have established that co-operative theory suggests the need to share the products of economic activity fairly. In this section I will explore what this implies for the way economic organisations are structured and managed. In a capitalist economy, production is carried out by enterprises usually called firms, which compete with each other and seek to maximise profits that are paid to those who have invested capital into the firm. They are managed hierarchically, with those higher up the hierarchy receiving a higher rate of pay. All of these characteristics of economic organisation are challenged by co-operative economics.

As we have seen, co-operative principles and values require a commitment to both equity and equality. Therefore, the hierarchical model is replaced by one in which all the members, consumers or workers who own the business should have an equal right to make decisions about how the firm operates. Many decisions are made on the basis of a democratic vote. For example, many co-operatives are run by boards elected by the employees who keep the business going on a day-to-day basis, while important decisions are made at an annual meeting which all member-employees are invited to attend. Similarly, financial co-operatives like credit unions or building societies make important decisions at the annual general meeting (AGM), and each person who has a loan or a deposit account with the co-operative is eligible to attend and vote.

Co-operatives also challenge the competitive drive at the heart of capitalism and the presumption that competition drives prices down and benefits consumers. A co-operator would ask, 'Who is bearing the costs for the lower price I have to pay?', recognising that this is usually done by the producer. As previously explained, co-operative economics challenges the way producers and consumers are pitted against each other.

Recalling the labour theory of value, co-operative economics requires that the value generated in a firm belongs to all employees equally. Rather than paying a share of profits to shareholders, who have not contributed labour but only capital to the firm, co-operatives generate surpluses, which are then either shared by the people who created them or re-invested in the business. Co-operatives are also committed to an equitable pay structure, with some retaining the original commitment to strictly equal pay. In some co-operatives, to avoid the distancing of managers from other staff, there is a rotation in tasks on a six-monthly or annual basis. This has the advantage that every employee understands the tasks of every other, giving a clearer sense of unified purpose to the firm as a whole.

The idea of balancing production and consumption also has important implications for the way firms are managed. The original model of the capitalist firm had a single owner or a partnership of a few entrepreneurs who owned the company and also ran it. The evolution of the company structure led to the separation of the owners of the firm, the 'shareholders', and the managers of the firm. It could no longer be assumed that their interests were aligned. Managers might make production or investment decisions that would enhance their power or increase their salaries but would not serve the interests of the shareholders.

This theory was first developed by Berle and Means (1932), who pointed out that the interests of shareholders and managers were in conflict. They argued that the 'modern' firm had to find a way to resolve that conflict, with both sides accepting what they defined as 'satisficing' rather than 'maximising' solutions. The negotiation to achieve a resolution can absorb time and energy that would be better spent improving the efficiency of the firm itself. In a recent study of co-operative enterprises in the finance sector, Sanchez Bajo and Roelants (2011) found that owners who are actively engaged in the firm improve the functioning of the firm compared to external shareholders.

In a workers' co-operative, as we have already discovered, there is no conflict between owners and producers since they are the same person: the employees own the firm. There are no external shareholders. Hence, the conflict between shareholders and managers evaporates, and no energy is wasted in resolving the tension. Co-operatives have the huge *advantage* of having their values and goals aligned, since they are established by the global co-operative movement of which the firms are members and who coordinate co-operative support and marketing on a global basis. At least in theory, and frequently also in practice, this means that the co-operative can focus only on the shared objectives. However, there is a danger that the highly engaged nature of its management process absorbs time in meetings where the worker-owners make decisions about strategy and the future direction of the firm.

A century ago, debates about the nature of production extended beyond the confines of the co-operatives themselves and were at the heart of the political debate in Europe's democracies. In Britain, the debate revolved around the guild socialists, who argued that workers should control their own workplaces and that these co-operatives should be at the heart of ethical local economies. Their opponents were the Fabians, who argued for national state control of industry supported by a strongly unionised workforce. G.D.H. Cole, who later wrote the history of their struggle, was a co-operative economist and explained that for the guild socialists:

> the 'workers control' they stood for was, above all else, control by the actual working group over the management of its own affairs within the framework of a wider control of policy formulated and executed as democratically as possible, and with the largest diffusion of responsibility and power.
>
> (Cole, 1960, pp. 246–247)

The battle was won by the Fabians, who became dominant in the Labour Party, which then proceeded to nationalise industry until this strategy was defeated by the revival of liberal values in economic and political life. This led to the privatisation of the industries that had once been managed for the public good.

One of the UK's leading retail companies – John Lewis – offers an interesting example of the benefits of a co-operatively owned enterprise. In this case the founder, Spedan Lewis, effectively gave his company to a trust whose mission is stated in its constitution as to achieve happiness for the company's employees. It suggests that this happiness depends on employees having satisfying jobs in a successful business. The company cannot make profits, but the surplus it generates is shared between the employees once a year through the payment of a dividend. John Lewis does not have all the features of a co-operative, since the employees are not the actual owners or the managers of the firm, but it certainly does not have any external shareholders. Employees are known as 'partners', and we can presume that the fact that they share in the value created by the business has a positive impact on their motivation. Although employees at John Lewis do not have the same power that they would as members of a co-operative, they do still have a role through their ability to elect 80% of the partnership council, which is the main decision-making body.

Trade from a co-operative perspective

In the first section, I outlined how co-operative economists try to find an ethical balance between the production and consumption sides of the economy. Nowhere is the evidence of a lack of balance more clear than in the global trading system. The neoclassical approach to trade is based on the 'theory of comparative advantage' developed by David Ricardo in the early 19th century.[4] This suggests that a country can benefit from trade even if it is less efficient in the production of all goods and services than the countries it is trading with. The first thing to say about this idea is that it is a theory. It has not been supported by empirical evidence, but made unchallengeable by constant repetition by those whose interests it serves. It entirely ignores the reason why the world's poorest countries have not grown rich in spite of being involved in a global trading system for at least the past 300 years: they have not been as powerful as those they are trading with. Whether through colonialism or the neo-colonialism of the World Trade Organization (WTO) and trade agreements, trade has led to the exploitation of the countries of the global South. This has benefited companies in the West that have organised the trade routes and the terms of trade and that dominate the market where traded goods are sold.

A brief history of the co-operative movement was offered earlier in this chapter. By the 1980s, The Co-operative was moving its way towards ethical trading as part of its 'co-operative difference' approach, emphasising the importance to its business of offering a fair price to producers and sharing surpluses with members. It began with Cafédirect, a fair-trade brand launched by a number of development charities, which the co-operative shops were the first to stock from May 1992. Fair trade is now a widely recognised and popular concept, but it is not so frequently understood that the co-operative principles make fair trade fair. Not only does it encapsulate the idea of fairness between producers and consumers but it also enables co-operative retailers to demonstrate commitment to the principle of favouring co-operatives above other forms of enterprise. Co-operatives can commit more clearly to ethical trade since they are not obliged to maximise profits and can also use their shops for educational purposes by labelling goods with information about the producers and making leaflets explaining the purpose of fair trade available to customers (Shaw, 2008). The Co-operative Group has also been clear about its future commitment: "Our goal is that, eventually all Co-op products from developing countries will be fairly traded and that fair trade ingredients are used more and more in our standard products" (Anderson, 2008). While fair trade does not have to be based on co-operative production, co-operatives can guarantee through their structure that no middlemen make profit without the need for further inspection or labelling.

Like co-operatives themselves, the range, scope and impact of the fair trade movement is often under-estimated. In reality it is one of the ethical success stories of the past thirty years and a living challenge to conventional economic theory that suggests consumers will always be driven to find the lowest price and that producers will succeed by competing with each other. The Fairtrade Foundation lists more than 4,000 products that are fairly traded, from bananas and coffee to flowers and even mobile phones. The idea of fair trade has now extended into the concept of demanding accountability for the supply chain. The ethical cosmetics firm Neal's Yard Remedies sources its ingredients so as to benefit local communities like the Samburu in Kenya who provide its frankincense. The higher prices they pay ensure fresh, clean water for the women who harvest the frankincense and enable their children to go to school. Monitoring of supply chains has also become a political matter, particularly in the case of precious stones or rare metals used in mobile phone manufacture which will soon need to be proved not to have funded conflicts.

Co-operation and the social good

Co-operatives are a unique form of business that, while seeking to be efficient and to serve their members, can also achieve a wider social good; indeed, unlike shareholder companies, that is an equally important part of their objectives. Co-operatives can play a particularly important role in alleviating poverty in the global South, both through expanding and supporting fair trade as already discussed, but also by directly reducing levels of poverty.

It was by 2015 that the United Nations had required the world to reach the Millennium Development Goals, ensuring that nobody in the world would suffer extreme poverty or lack basic education, health care or water. While progress has not been as widespread as had been initially hoped, it is clear that co-operatives have played an important part in what has been achieved so far. Although the World Bank has continued to sing its siren song about the value of trade liberalisation and the spread of free markets, it is clear that ethical trade has been most successful in attacking global poverty. As was highlighted in Andrew Bibby and Linda Shaw's 2005 report:

> It is heartening that the United Nations and its agencies have already on several occasions acknowledged the contribution which co-operatives can make. The UN General Assembly resolution 54/123 emphasised the importance of co-operative organisations in social development, poverty reduction, employment creation and participatory development. Subsequent to this, the UN Secretariat issued a set of *Co-operatives in Social Development* Guidelines (2001). These recognise the 'co-operative movement as a distinct and major stakeholder in both national and international affairs'. They advise member states to adopt a policy framework to recognise co-operatives as legal entities and to give co-operative organisations and institutions equality in relation to other associations and institutions.
>
> (Bibby and Shaw, 2005)

This unique organisational structure not only ensures an equitable distribution of the proceeds of work, but it also enables co-operatives to prioritise social and ecological value above the maximisation of profit. As an example, a profit-driven firm would create products with short life-spans so that we need to boost their profits by buying again and again; a co-operative firm could rather design products that achieve social ends, such the minimisation of resources use or ease of mending, without fear of pressure from shareholders (Cato, 2012).

From a green perspective, another benefit of co-operatives is that they are not focused on growth. This is especially important in a world where economic growth is putting increasing pressure on the environment. For a capitalist firm, growth implies more market control and higher profits and is thus a central goal. For a co-operative, which needs to maintain a strong relationship with its members and/or workers, a larger size can be quite challenging. It makes it harder to maintain a consistent focus and to ensure that the views of all members are taken into account.

The role of co-operatives in meeting needs that the market is not supplying has also enabled co-operatives to make an important contribution to the green transition, especially in the area of electricity generation. Denmark has seen a huge expansion of its wind generation focused on local community ownership within a framework of strong government support (Cumbers, 2012). The German *Energiewende* has also been driven by a tenfold expansion in electricity-generating co-operatives during the past decade. In a market dominated by large generators focused on fossil fuels, consumers have decided to meet their own need for green electricity by setting up their own energy co-operatives, enabling them to reap the benefit as well as demonstrate their commitment to a sustainable future.

Some co-operative economists also argue that this form of economic organisation can offer more in terms of productivity and innovation. Margaret Levenstein of the

University of Michigan and her colleagues have carried out an analysis of historical data on investment and innovation in Cleveland, Ohio in the 1930s (Lamoreaux et al., 2004), which was at the cutting edge of technological development at this time. They found that the innovation investment was diverted into speculative activity as the stock-market bubble developed. When it crashed, all local investment was lost, and the local economy never recovered its cutting edge. The productivity advantages of co-operatives are summed up as follows:

> All enterprises need employees, customers and investors in order to function in a market economy. These stakeholders have competing economic interests in the enterprise: employees want higher wages, customers want cheaper products and investors want bigger returns. The aim of co-operatives is to reconcile the competing interests of stakeholders by operating within an ethical code of values and principles, where interests are aligned in pursuit of a common social purpose. Co-operatives must also produce wealth that can be shared by all the stakeholders. The best measure of this wealth-creating ability is productivity not profitability. Higher productivity benefits all the stakeholders.
>
> (Brown, 2004, pp. 24–25)

The final social spillover from co-operative organisations comes in the form of the changes co-operators discover in their lives as they take more control over their economic destiny. From understanding how to run a meeting to being able to draw up business plans and spreadsheets, working in a co-operative business helps to build a wide range of skills. The co-operative values and principles also encourage co-operatives to make a positive social impact in their communities. This goes beyond corporate social responsibility (CSR) and also encourages those who work in co-operative firms to re-evaluate their role in society, often leading to volunteering activity or wider political engagement.

In summary, co-operatives are a really exciting form of economic organisation that is distinct in a number of ways from capitalist enterprises. They prioritise respecting producers, consumers and the environment, and their very structure resists the exploitation that defaces much of the global economy. They give employees and customers direct power to influence how the business works that goes beyond customer power or ethical shopping. They are found in every country in the world and in vastly different political and economic systems. Co-operatives represent a quiet and inconspicuous way to achieve an alternative and fairer economy that does not require a head-on assault on capitalism and are therefore well worth investigating.

Notes

1 The difference between a surplus and a profit is really only one of perspective. Both represent income made over and above the costs required to create that income (wages,

investment in productive capacity, marketing, etc.). Both profits and surpluses can be reinvested in the business or paid to employees as bonuses or external shareholders as dividends. Generally, shareholder companies use the term 'profit', whereas co-operatives and not-for-profit companies prefer to use the term 'surplus'.

2　The full list can be found here: www.co-operative.coop/corporate/aboutus/the-co-operative-group-values-and-principles/.

3　A fictitious commodity is something that is treated as a commodity within the context of a capitalist, market economy but which has an origin and essence that transcends this role; it is therefore denigrated and prevented from achieving its true essence by this limitation imposed by the market system of economic organisation.

4　The theory of comparative advantage suggests that countries should focus their production on the good or service that they produce most efficiently. If each country does this, all countries will benefit from trade, even those who produce all goods less efficiently than other countries.

References

Anderson, M. (2009), 'The British Fair Trade Movement, 1960–2000: A New Form of Global Citizenship?', Unpublished PhD Thesis, The University of Birmingham.

Beecher, J., Cato, M. S. and Weir, N. (2012), 'The Resilience of Co-operative Food Networks: A Case-Study of Stroud', in: McDonnell, D., Macknight, E. and Donnelly, H. (eds.), *The Co-Operative Model in Practice*, Edinburgh: Co-operative Enterprise Scotland, pp. 55–66.

Berle, A. and Means, G. (1932), *The Modern Corporation and Private Property*, New York: Transaction.

Bibby, A. and Shaw, L. (2005), *Making a Difference: Co-Operative Solutions to Global Poverty*, Manchester: Co-Operative College.

Bickle, R. and Cato, M. S. (2008), *New Views of Society: Robert Owen for the 21st Century*, Glasgow: Scottish Left Review Press.

Brown, J. (2004), *Co-operative Capital: A New Approach to Investment in Co-operatives and Other Forms of Social Enterprise*, Manchester, UK: Co-operative Action.

Cato, M. S. (2012), 'The Green Economy: Why Ownership and Control Matter', *Journal of Co-Operative Studies*, Vol. 45, No. 1, pp. 61–68.

Cole, G. D. H. (1953–1960), *Socialist Thought*, London: Macmillan; the volumes consulted here are vol i, *The Forerunners 1789–1850* (1954), vol ii, *Marxism and Anarchism 1850–1890* (1957), and vol iii, *The Second International 1889–1914* (1960).

Cumbers, A. (2012), *Reclaiming Public Ownership: Making Space for Economic Democracy*, London: Zed.

International Co-operative Alliance (2015), 'World Co-Operative Monitor: Exploring the Co-Operative Economy', retrieved from: http://monitor.coop/sites/default/files/WCM_2015%20WEB.pdf.

Lamoreaux, N. R., Levenstein, M. and Sokoloff, K. (2004), 'Financing Invention During the Second Industrial Revolution: Cleveland, Ohio 1870–1920', NBER Working Paper 10923.

Novkovic, S. and Webb, T. (2014), *Co-Operatives in a Post-Growth Era: Creating Co-Operative*, Economics Paperback, London: Zed.

Polanyi, K. (2011[1944]), *The Great Transformation: The Political and Economic Origins of Our Time*, Boston, MA: Beacon Press.

Sanchez Bajo, C. and Roelants, B. (2011), *Capital and the Debt Trap: Learning from Cooperatives in the Global Crisis*, Basingstoke, UK: Palgrave Macmillan.

Shaw, L. (2008), 'Owen and Food', in: Bickle, R. and Cato, M. S. (eds.), *New Views of Society: Robert Owen for the 21st Century*, Glasgow: Scottish Left Review Press, pp. 14–28.

Smith, R. (2011), 'Boundarity Rationality: Towards a Theory of the Co-Operative Firm', Unpublished Paper, Cardiff Institute for Cooperative Studies, Cardiff Metropolitan University.

9 Ecological economics

From nature to society

Clive L. Spash and Viviana Asara

Introduction

Ecological Economics represents a line of thought relating to energy and the environment in economics, which can be traced back well into the 1800s (Martinez-Alier, 1990). More generally, it places economics in the context of themes that have been central concerns for humanity since the ancient Greeks. These include the limits to wealth creation, the meaning of the good life, how to achieve well-being individually and socially, ethics and behaviour, the epistemology of value, and the psychological and social impact of ostentatious consumption. The current movement is founded upon the concerns of the 1960s and early 1970s for limits to growth (Meadows et al., 1972), the study of the flow of energy and materials in the economy based upon the work of Georgescu-Roegen (1971), and the re-conceptualisation of 'externalities' as pervasive social cost-shifting and an integral part of modern economic activity (Kapp, 1950, 1978). However, past writers, expressing such a social and ecological critique of economics, failed to create a collective formally institutionalised academic base. The more formal establishment of associations and journals only occurred in the late 1980s and early 1990s, in part due to the growing criticism of and dissension within orthodox environmental economics (Spash, 1999, 2011).

In Barcelona in 1987, at a meeting hosted by Joan Martinez-Alier, the International Society for Ecological Economics (ISEE) was born, and the first issue of the journal *Ecological Economics* appeared in 1989. The basic conceptualisation of reality (i.e., the ontological presupposition) that explicitly recognises the economy as embedded within a larger ecological system was a common foundation for participants. This self-evident reality was and remains denied and/or ignored by all mainstream economics and heterodox theories as well. Economies are studied as if they were independent of the biophysical systems within which they are embedded and upon which they are totally dependent.

Studying the relationships between the economy and the environment is an optional extra for economists, and a minority pursuit. A range of economic approaches maintain as a common utopian vision the growth economy and the core recommendation for success being an ever-growing material and energy throughput.[1] This has become enshrined as a doctrine of faith at the heart of the modern industrial society: 'thou shalt grow thy economy'. The basic assumption that remains dominant amongst economists, of all sorts, is that the economic system is physically isolated (i.e., has no energy or material exchange with any other system) and can meaningfully be studied as such. In fact, this is neither the biophysical reality in which humans actually live, nor a valid assumption upon which to study the conditions that enable the reproduction of economic activity and society.

In contrast to all other economic approaches, the fundamental connection to biophysical reality has been at the heart of ecological economics. However, what has been inadequately addressed is the connection to society within which economies are also embedded. The result of not emphasising this explicitly has been to accept the adoption of formalistic approaches to combining environmental concerns with the economic. In this respect many ecological economists have maintained a concept of a formal economy that basically is regarded as efficiently allocating resources. This approach is no different from the resource and environmental economists who constitute a sub-disciplinary field of neoclassical economics. Difficulties then arise in differentiating between mainstream and heterodox economic approaches to the environment, especially when the latter merely add more stringent side constraints to the same models. In addition, systemic criticism of the existing economic arrangements in society have been lacking, e.g., corporate power, price setting markets, capital accumulation, the role of the State, the military-industrial complex. This is in part because natural scientists and neoclassical economists studying environment-economy interactions have had little or no concern for social reality.

Addressing the economy as a price-making market system and unifying economics under deductive mathematical modelling has involved the conversion of all entities into objects. Land, labour, and capital take the commodity form and become mechanical cogs in the economic machine. Hence economics conceptualises the world as human capital, social capital, cultural capital, and natural capital. This conversion into capital is a prime example of failure in scientific analysis, which needs to relate to the qualities of the actual objects of study (i.e., humans, society, culture, and Nature). Yet, as Karl Polanyi (1944) detailed long ago, this move is also an essential part of creating a real social structure that facilitates and enables the operation of the actual price-making market economy. What should then be evident is that the relationship between economic systems and their enabling social structures has been wilfully neglected and purposefully excluded from the analysis. The failure of the environmental critique of price-setting markets and the growth economy has been to focus on the exploitation of Nature alone, rather than recognising the commonalities with social exploitation that would have raised concerns over social structure.

Thus, the aim of Social Ecological Economics is to rethink both mainstream and heterodox economics in their common caricature of economic potential and the dismissal of the possibility of alternative systems. Both typically adopt a utopian vision of economic growth and are subject to the critique of being divorced from reality. However, this is not to deny that some branches (e.g., evolutionary, critical institutional, feminist, social, neo-Marxist) of the heterodoxy hold more hope for a new economics because they are already aware of the failures of some aspects of the current system. An important concern here is the ontology (i.e., view of reality) adopted by the heterodoxy. For example, a fundamental point of departure from the mainstream is the recognition that the economy is an open system – requiring other systems for its inputs and disposal of its outputs. Still, the lack of attention to the social and ecological reality in which economic systems operate remains common, and as long as this situation persists, economists will continue in their failure to understand why humanity is facing a major social ecological transformation. Indeed, that transformation will then more likely be to a worse not better world, and reached by disaster and not design.

In this chapter, we briefly outline the Ecological Economics critique of economic thinking. In addition to the critique based on understanding biophysical reality, we emphasise placing economic understanding in the context of the necessary social structures. We then look at how Ecological Economics became a contended field of knowledge facing internal divisions between New Resource Economists, New Environmental Pragmatists and Social Ecological Economists. Only the latter is concerned with rethinking economics. That raises the need for new ways of thinking about interacting and stratified systems. Along the way, Critical Realism is introduced as being the best available philosophy of science to inform the foundation of a new Social Ecological Economic understanding. Finally, we turn to some future directions in which research needs to go, and mention the correspondence with the concerns of the degrowth movement, while also highlighting the threats to democratic aspirations of humanity.

The content and meaning of an ecological economics

The incorporation of the Laws of Thermodynamics into economics in the early 1970s was key to the revitalised understanding of economics that became Ecological Economics. The First Law of Thermodynamics states that mass, like energy, can be neither created nor destroyed in an isolated system. Strictly, Earth is an open system (exchanging both materials and energy with its wider surroundings), but is in effect a closed system because there is little significant materials exchange. Mainly Earth exchanges energy with the solar system.

This means that human activities can transform but not destroy materials. An economic system that is based upon material throughput creates as much mass of waste as the resources it uses. These wastes go into Earth's environmental systems, which must then assimilate them, if they can. Where assimilation fails, transformation occurs, with change subject to irreversibility and ecosystems being degraded in their functional capacity. This is a direct consequence of the First Law of Thermodynamics. Much emphasis in Ecological Economics has been placed on the scale of throughput activity and the need to constrain this (e.g., steady-state, degrowth), but the quality of materials being returned to the environment is also crucial to the impacts and resulting changes. This means that the type of human activities, and not just their scale, should be a central concern (e.g., toxic waste, radiation, genetic modification, microwave transmission, plastics).

The Second Law of Thermodynamics states that energy changes quality from useful (low entropy) to less useful (high entropy), heading towards an equilibrium of dissipation and all energy being of the same quality (in an isolated system). This process is irreversible unless energy is added from another system. Most notable amongst those exploring and exposing these issues and detailing their economic implications was Georgescu–Roegen (1971, 1975). The entropy law has been taken to imply absolute constraints on economic systems. That is, there are basic biophysical limits on what humans can do. Available highly concentrated (low entropy) mineral resources are limited, and available useful (low entropy) energy comes from such minerals, the Sun and the movement of the planets. The modern economy and the associated society is built upon and sustained by the first source, namely, fossil fuels.

Georgescu–Roegen (1975) extrapolated from his interpretation of classical entropy as to the desirability of reduced growth and avoiding luxury items constituted of metals, which future generations would need for basic food production. The concept of social metabolism brings forward the work connected to an entropic view on the economy. Social metabolism addresses the biophysical exchange of materials and energy flows between human systems and Nature, taking also into consideration the causal mechanisms of their patterns and dynamics (Krausmann, 2017). A human body needs a continuous throughput of materials in order to survive – oxygen, food, water – which then are returned to the environment in the form of urea, excrement, carbon dioxide, methane, heat and so on. Similarly, a social economic system needs flows of material and energy for the production and reproduction of its biophysical structures: not only food and water, but also fuel, minerals, and raw materials. All the material and energy that a society extracts from the environment will undergo a transformation and will result in the production of waste.

While the concept of social metabolism can be traced to the works of Marx, it was reintroduced in the 1960s, and has been developed since in the field of industrial ecology. The conceptual basis derives from the 'materials balance theory' of the 1970s, which traces the resources input to an economic system, through the production and consumption processes, to their final destination as wastes and emissions. That is, all resource inputs are traced to their equivalent pollution outputs. The implications of the materials balance work in conjunction with general equilibrium modelling is that all the prices in the economy are incorrect in terms of efficiency because everything has an associated environmental externality.

Social metabolism research over recent decades has revealed how industrialisation created a metabolic transition, that is an unprecedented rise in metabolic rates (the rate of throughput), and a shift to a low share of renewable biomass and a large amount of materials stored in stocks of built infrastructure (Spash and Schandl, 2009). It also provides a basis for understanding the material and energy basis for the reproduction of a variety of different human systems at different scales (e.g., nation States, cities, households). Technological optimists and those hoping to maintain the current economic system unchanged hope that economic growth can continue while material and energy inputs decline. Absolute dematerialisation or decoupling (divorcing economic growth from material consumption) is not occurring, and cases where it has been claimed empirically have proven to be instances of the delocalisation of production (e.g., offshoring resource intensive and polluting production activities). Another popular way to try to dismiss the relevance of biophysical reality is to claim the monetary value of output – typically measured as Gross Domestic Product (GDP) – is increasing relative to the use of resources. However, this relative decoupling is rather meaningless as far as impacts on ecosystems and social exploitation are concerned. Indeed the value of GDP can increase as more pollution requires clean-up and more people get sick; there is nothing better for GDP growth than a good disaster. As resources become scarcer, mainstream economics predicts their value should increase, which would, ceteris paribus, also mean GDP increasing in value for no change in material inputs.

Another reason why absolute (i.e., input per unit of total output) decoupling fails to materialise is what has become known as the rebound effect or Jevons' Paradox (named after the economist William Stanley Jevons). This explains the counterbalancing of efficiency gains in resource use, due to technological improvements, by the increase in the rate of consumption of the same resource. Basically, as prices fall due to efficiency gains, consumers can consume more. For example, car engines today are far more efficient than they were in the 1970s, but car ownership has increased, people drive more, they take more journeys as individuals (no passengers) and overall consume more fuel. The engine that made cars cheaper and more fuel efficient did not save any fuel on aggregate. Thus, despite improvements in material use and productivity gains, growth in materials use continues to be a general feature of economic expansion in production and consumption.

From the ecological to the social

The original thesis of limits to economic growth (Meadows et al., 1972) was presented as a scenario analysis that combined analysis of five causal mechanisms: population growth, accelerating industrialisation, adequacy of agricultural production, depletion of natural resources, and pollution. The scenarios resulted in collapse despite a wide variety of assumptions, but also the text mentioned briefly the expectation of social limits arriving before the biophysical ones. That is, war, breakdown of civil society and inequity would be likely before resources were exhausted.

In Ecological Economics, the limits to growth have also been highlighted by different kinds of social economists working from a range of perspectives: institutional, evolutionary, Marxist, sociological, eco-feminist, science and technology studies. Their concerns as Ecological Economists were at least partially inspired by previous criticisms of economic growth from within the economic profession, e.g., Karl William Kapp, Ezra. J. Mishan and John Kenneth Galbraith. Part of that critique concerns the fallacy of the sovereign consumer and the role of corporate capitalism in creating the illusion of an affluent society. This was the realisation of the American dream where private affluence for the few is bought at the cost of public squalor for the many. This led beyond bio-physical limits into the realisation that there were also social limits to growth, as had been emphasised by Fred Hirsch (1977).

Ecological Marxism is articulated along three main lines of thinking (Douai, 2017):

i   the metabolic character of human labour, producing since the industrial era a 'meta-bolic rift', or a rift in the metabolic exchange between humanity and nature, which leads to a failure to sustain the condition of the earth's reproduction (Foster, 2011);

ii the double character of the commodity as use-value and exchange-value, with the latter increasingly dominant. Use value is associated with fundamental human needs, while exchange value is oriented to the pursuit of profit, creating a contradiction between capitalist production and the natural conditions of production (ibid);

iii the ecological contradiction of capitalism founded for example on the double char-acter of the capitalist labour process (as a fundamental dimension of social life and as a capitalist factor or production), or in the antagonistic relationship between the forces and relations of production and the conditions of production, the latter being the "non-capitalist social domains and publically provided infrastructures" that "fur-nish the necessary material and social conditions for commodity production, market exchange and capitalist accumulation" (O'Connor, 1994, p. 106).

There are a range of contributors who have been active in discussing the relationship between Marxism/socialism and the political economy of Nature, and within the Euro-pean Society for Ecological Economics there was early on a political ecology element (for references, see Spash and Ryan, 2012).

Ecofeminism has contributed to the analysis by pointing out that the labour theory of value downplays the reproductive dimension. That is, there has been a failure to realise how relations of production are reliant on a labour surplus through the generation of gender exploitation in the domestic sphere (Salleh, 2017). An 'embodied materialism' is 'materialist' for endorsing the basic tools of a Marxist sociology, and 'embodied' because it is able to acknowledge the non-monetised regenerative activities performed by 'every-day care labour' (mostly performed by women) that are necessary for everyday life and for the global economy to function. In this light, eco-sufficiency refers to the capacity of this socially reproductive labour for provisioning without the production of social, embodied or ecological debt (ibid).

More generally, social economists emphasise human motivation and behaviour within social structures (e.g., organisations, culture). Critical institutional economists engaging in ecological economics emphasise formal rules, norms, and conventions or practices (Vatn, 2017). Current global environmental governance and patterns are dependent on global resource and power inequalities, which should make the study of power and conflict a central aspect of analysis. Mainstream economics totally fails on this front, and the spread of liberal and neoliberal idealism into neoclassical and macro economics has meant devotion to the single idea of individual autonomy and the denigration of planning and governance by government.

This exclusive emphasis on the individual and neglect of power means a total absence in economic analysis of the modern corporation and a failure to account for the rise of the banking and finance sectors. Methodological individualism adds to the poverty of analytical ability by denying the existence of society as something more than a bunch of individuals and as something epistemologically reducible to the individual. Society, understood as having emergent properties, is more complex but more realistic and meaningful. It also raises deep concerns over the dynamics of the interactions between economic and social institutions. As Polanyi (1944) explained, the modern market economy is a specific type and set of institutional arrangements, which requires a market society.

Divisions in the field

Although Ecological Economics as a modern movement started at the basic level of trying to combine models from ecology and economics, developing a heterodox interdisciplinary research field with a distinct methodology and approach to ecological and social economic interactions was not on everyone's agenda and has involved conflict. Lack of attention to the theoretical foundations of Ecological Economics has left it in a precarious and epistemologically confused position (Spash, 2012). More particularly, transdisciplinarity and methodological pluralism have been taken as core ideas by many in Ecological Economics, but with the result that critical theoretical reflection has been lacking. Association to mainstream economic ideas and incorporation of economic formalism have had severe impacts, from marginalisation of anything heterodox to the constitution of a confusing mix of papers regularly published in the journal *Ecological Economics*. In the extreme, this has been used by mainstream economists to reduce Ecological Economics to a subfield of orthodox environmental economics, as found in the standard classification system of the *Journal of Economic Literature*. Ecological Economics is populated by a variety of contributors and affiliates, who can be separated by their theoretical and ideological positions into three main camps: the new resource economists, the new environmental pragmatists, and social ecological economists (Spash, 2013).

New resource economists are embedded within free-market ideology and mainstream price theory, a utilitarian approach framed within a fact-value dichotomy, and the belief that 'getting prices right' is the key way forward for solving environmental problems. Efforts are taken to include ecosystem functions in economic models, within a framework of efficient and optimal resource use. In terms of methodology, the key approach is to use mathematical formalism to create abstract models, which are then meant to explain aspects of reality and make predictions about the future to advise policy.

New environmental pragmatists have been prevalent in Ecological Economics and, more generally, represent a mode of thinking that has spread throughout the environmental movement. They are focused on pushing methods and concepts because they are deemed to be effective under current political conditions and economic institutions (i.e., those of neoliberalism and capitalism). These pragmatists want to sell their environmental message in an appropriately marketable form that is acceptable to political, business and financial elites. In doing so, they buy into the methodology and ideology of commodifying, quantifying and pricing Nature. This form of pragmatic drive can be seen in a variety of work and the use of concepts such as ecosystem services valuation, natural capital, green accounting, carbon trading, and biodiversity offsets and banking. The distinguishing feature of new environmental pragmatism is the lack of concern for theoretical rigour, especially in the social sciences, and prioritisation of methods to achieve supposed 'solutions' on purely instrumental grounds. Environmentalism is then a practical problem solving activity, not a fundamental critique of the dominant structure of political economy and its treatment of human relationships with Nature.

Social Ecological Economics is distinct from the other two main camps in aiming to address fundamental flaws of the existing economic orthodoxy, from consumer sovereignty to corporate structure and power politics. One crucial aspect is the acceptance of the ever changing world in which humans live, rather than pretending there is inherent stability and equilibrium. This perspective builds on the understanding of dynamics, emergence and systems change that can be found in a variety of work, including that on ecosystems, co-evolutionary development and complexity. The approach is inherently interdisciplinary, linking economics with a range of academic disciplines such as social psychology, sociology, applied philosophy, geography, politics, and the natural sciences. The potential for Social Ecological Economics is then in terms of helping develop a progressive social and environmental movement built on interdisciplinary research. Interdisciplinarity avoids the potential for an approach skating over the content of other disciplines, as too often seems to arise under references to transdisciplinarity as employed by the New Environmental Pragmatists.

A foundational aspect for Social Ecological Economics in terms of epistemology is a synthesis of realism and weak constructivism and the rejection of pluralist eclecticism. The approach rejects the scientific reduction of the natural environment to its physical characteristics and the strong constructivist position, which denies biophysical constraints on social life. Social Ecological Economics has a philosophy of science that is compatible with Critical Realism, which also aims to provide an understanding of the interaction between physical and social systems (Spash, 2012).

Critical Realism accepts that we can never demonstrate that we have discovered the truth, even if we have (fallibilism), but does not reject the idea of there being an underlying objective reality. The description under critical realism is of an ordered hierarchy of sciences at the structural level. There is real (ontological) difference in the strata, so they are not regarded as just cognitively (epistemologically) convenient. The real distinctions between the strata and their irreducibility of one to another (contra reductionism) are used to explain differences between the various sciences and the reason for a plurality of sciences to exist. So, for example, because everything is governed by the laws of physics, all biological entities are physical but not vice versa. Therefore biological sciences are embedded within the physical and, likewise, the social within the biological, and the formal economy within the social. At the level of structural mechanisms there is a one-way hierarchy. This type of embeddedness is one of the key messages Ecological Economists have been at pains to communicate, and especially that the economy is embedded in the Natural environment and subject to the Laws of Thermodynamics. Yet, embeddedness should not be confused with reductionism. Biology cannot be understood from physics, nor a human from studying cells, nor the social from the economic (Spash, 2012, 2015).

Social science, including economics, can be differentiated on a substantive basis from the natural sciences because it involves (contra Hume) an inseparability of facts and values. Understanding social phenomena (e.g., unemployment) requires addressing the real structural causes (e.g., financial institutions, government policy, world markets) and prevalent ideas. Those ideas appear as social attitudes and political behaviour. Thus, explanations arising from a social scientific study entail criticism of some ideas in society. Furthermore, there is often a functional relationship between organisations that cause false beliefs and beliefs about those organisations. False beliefs may be spread in order to preserve an organisation, its power and associated institutions. Thus, the rhetoric of the liberating character of 'free-markets' and benefits of material growth may be used by corporations and governments extracting resources, dislocating indigenous populations and creating environmental destruction. In such cases, to propound the truth is not just to criticise, but to undermine the institution. Explanations of social institutions are a precondition of criticising and changing them, and sometimes the critique will begin the work of their subversion. Open realisation and acceptance of this position makes Social Ecological Economics far more radical than orthodox economics, which pretends to give objective, value-free advice while actually supporting the existing institutional structures.

Future directions

Social Ecological Economics is concerned about the policy consequences of its arguments, openly claims ethical positions rather than neutrality, accepts that values can be disputed and incommensurable, recognises distributional issues (e.g., inequity) as a primary issue, and is concerned with the ecologically based needs to address the scale and quality of human activity. Distributional concerns and a critique of the growth imperative have recently given rise to an emerging field of research envisioning a social ecological transformation, connecting more particularly to the degrowth critique and increasing realisation of the necessity of envisioning a post-growth society.

Building on Ecological Economics, the degrowth critique has argued that growth is not only ecologically unsustainable but also unjust and unfeasible in the long term, and is no longer improving human well-being (Asara et al., 2013). Degrowth could be defined as a democratically led redistributive downscaling of production and consumption in industrialised countries and of the role of markets as a central organising principle of human life, as a means to achieve environmental sustainability, social justice and well-being (Sekulova et al., 2013). Degrowth has been argued to involve a social ecological transformation (Asara et al., 2015). The critique is of policies that: recommend marginal adjustments to economic and social systems in response to crises, describe transition as maintaining pre-existing economic capital accumulating trajectories, and fail to question the hegemonic neoliberal mode of governance. The concept of transformation implies the need to go beyond simply protesting against business-as-usual and to actively create new meanings and social practices. This requires research into alternative economic modes of production, political institutions, ideologies, and societal norms. Transformations involve multiple scales of governance and system levels, from the local to the regional, national, and international.

Social Ecological Economics raises concerns over the meaning of democracy. Much of the environmental movement, including degrowth, emphasises a vision of democracy with participation, decentralised institutions, local production, and grassroots activism. This leaves open questions about coordination between spatially divided institutions and governance at other levels, besides the local. A research agenda involving political institutional analysis is required to address the conditions necessary to achieve democracy without a capital accumulating regime. Global processes spreading the institutions of neoliberal political economy, along with the creation of fictitious commodities (e.g., carbon as a tradable permit) and the spread of military intervention and strengthening of 'security' measures, point to society going in the opposite direction. These are the institutions of competition and domination.

Therein also lies the major challenge for anyone seriously concerned about the current direction of humanity. The economic system that has been established is one in which inequity is created and reinforced, resources are used in vast quantities by a minority, social and environmental costs are shifted onto the innocent and powerless, and all the time most economists talk about none of this but only efficiency. That efficiency is only one amongst many competing possible goals, and is itself a contentious basis for evaluation of economic systems and their performance, does not even appear to be in the universe of thought for most economists. This engineering mentality to life has wiped out the ethical approach to economics that once gave it some meaning.

The economy, understood as a means of provision and transfer of resources, neither requires efficiency nor does it work on the basis of efficiency today. There is nothing efficient in mass consumerism, conspicuous consumption, built-in obsolescence, the fashion society, competition, environmental degradation, and destruction or resource wars, let alone the multi-national corporation. The concept is often totally vacuous because there is no judgement as to what makes an action meaningful, let alone an ethical use of resources.

Conclusions

The field of Ecological Economics covers biology, ecology, thermodynamics, well-being, consumption, future generations, environmental values and ethics, uncertainty and ignorance, science policy, participation, and deliberation (see original works by various authors collected together in four volumes by Spash, 2009). This overview chapter gives a flavour of this content and does not attempt to be comprehensive. (For a recent collection of 50 articles, see Spash, 2017).

The basic ontology of Ecological Economics emphasises the stratification of reality. This means, at the most general level, that any economic system is embedded in a natural system. The fact that humans are bound within the structure of Nature, despite their innovative activities, means there are fundamental and foundational limits to the material and energy-based growth of any and all economic systems. This highlights the need for anyone concerned with the maintenance and stability of an economic system to address both the scale and type of economic activity.

In addition, the relationship of economies to societies is something social economists have emphasised but which has been too often neglected by environmentalists and is excluded from mainstream economics and all approaches based upon methodological individualism. The need of the market economy to convert society to a market society then has ongoing repercussions. That another economy and society are just as feasible and viable is at the heart of rethinking economics.

Note

1   Throughput is the term used to refer to the flow of material and energy through a system that maintains a given state of that system (e.g., the biological metabolism of an animal). Economic systems are then regarded as having a social metabolism (see Krausmann, 2017); discussed later in this chapter.

References cited

Asara, V., Otero, I., Demaria, F. and Corbera, E. (2015), 'Socially Sustainable Degrowth as a Social-Ecological Transformation: Repoliticizing Sustainability', *Sustainability Science*, Vol. 10, pp. 375–384.

Asara, V., Profumi, E. and Kallis, G. (2013), 'Degrowth, Democracy and Autonomy', *Environmental Values*, Vol. 22, pp. 217–239.

Douai, A. (2017), 'Ecological Marxism and ecological economics', in: Spash, C. L. (ed.), *Routledge Handbook of Ecological Economics: Nature and Society*, pp. 57–66, Abingdon: Routledge.

Foster, J. B. (2011), 'The Ecology of Marxian Political Economy', *Monthly Review*, Vol. 63, pp. 1–16.

Georgescu-Roegen, N. (1971), *The Entropy Law and the Economic Process*, Cambridge, MA: Harvard University Press.

Georgescu-Roegen, N. (1975), 'Energy and Economic Myths', *Southern Economic Journal*, Vol. 41, pp. 347–381.

Hirsch, F. (1977), *Social Limits to Growth*, London: Routledge and Kegan Paul Ltd.

Kapp, K. W. (1950), *The Social Costs of Private Enterprise*, New York: Shocken.

Kapp, K. W. (1978), *The Social Costs of Business Enterprise*, Nottingham: Spokesman.

Krausmann, F. (2017), 'Social Metabolism', in: Spash, C. L. (ed.), *Routledge Handbook of Ecological Economics: Nature and Society*, pp. 108–118, Abingdon: Routledge.

Martinez-Alier, J. (1990), *Ecological Economics: Energy, Environment and Society*, Oxford: Basil Blackwell.

Meadows, D. H., Meadows, D. L., Randers, J. and Behrens, W. W. III (1972), *The Limits to Growth*, London: Pan.

O'Connor, M. (1994), 'The Second Contradiction of Capitalism', *Capitalism Nature Socialism*, Vol. 5, pp. 105–114.

Polanyi, K. (1944), *The Great Transformation*, New York: Toronto: Rinehart & Company Inc.

Salleh, A. (2017), 'Ecofeminism', in: Spash, C. L. (ed.), *Routledge Handbook of Ecological Economics: Nature and Society*', pp. 48–56, Abingdon: Routledge.

Sekulova, F., Kallis, G., Rodriguez-Labajos, B. and Schneider, F. (2013), 'Degrowth: From Theory to Practice', *Journal of Cleaner Production*, Vol. 38, pp. 1–6.

Spash, C. L. (1999), 'The Development of Environmental Thinking in Economics', *Environmental Values*, Vol. 8, pp. 413–435.

Spash, C. L. (ed.) (2009), *Ecological Economics: Critical Concepts in the Environment*, 4 Volumes, London: Routledge.

Spash, C. L. (2011), 'Social Ecological Economics: Understanding the Past to See the Future', *American Journal of Economics and Sociology*, Vol. 70, pp. 340–375.

Spash, C. L. (2012), 'New Foundations for Ecological Economics', *Ecological Economics*, Vol. 77, pp. 36–47.

Spash, C. L. (2013), 'The Shallow or the Deep Ecological Economics Movement?', *Ecological Economics*, Vol. 93, pp. 351–362.

Spash, C. L. (2015), 'The Content, Direction and Philosophy of Ecological Economics', in: Martínez, A. and Muradian, R. (eds.), *Handbook of Ecological Economics*, Cheltenham: Edward Elgar, pp. 26–47.

Spash, C. L. (ed.) (2016), *Routledge Handbook of Ecological Economics: Nature and Society*, London: Routledge.

Spash, C. L. and Ryan, A. (2012), 'Economic Schools of Thought on the Environment: Investigating Unity and Division', *Cambridge Journal of Economics*, Vol. 36, pp. 1091–1121.

Spash, C. L. and Schandl, H. (2009), 'Challenges for Post Keynesian Growth Theory: Utopia Meets Environmental and Social Reality', in: Holt, R. P. F., Spash, C. L. and Pressman, S. (eds.), *Post Keynesian and Ecological Economics: Confronting Environmental Issues*, Cheltenham: Edward Elgar, pp. 47–77.

Vatn, A. (2017), 'Critical Institutional Economics', in: Spash, C. L. (ed.), *Routledge Handbook of Ecological Economics: Nature and Society*, Abingdon: Routledge, pp. 29–38.

Further reading

Georgescu-Roegen, N. (1971), *The Entropy Law and the Economic Process*. Cambridge, MA: Harvard University Press.

Kapp, K. W. (1978), *The Social Costs of Business Enterprise*, Nottingham: Spokesman.

Martinez-Alier, J. (1990), *Ecological Economics: Energy, Environment and Society*. Oxford, UK: Basil Blackwell.

Røpke, I. (2004), 'The Early History of Modern Ecological Economics', *Ecological Economics*, Vol. 50, Nos. 3–4, pp. 293–314.

Røpke, I. (2005), 'Trends in the Development of Ecological Economics From the Late 1980s to the Early 2000s', *Ecological Economics*, Vol. 55, No. 2, pp. 262–290.

Spash, C. L. (1999), 'The Development of Environmental Thinking in Economics', *Environmental Values*, Vol. 8, No. 4, pp. 413–435.

Spash, C. L. (ed.) (2009), *Ecological Economics: Critical Concepts in the Environment*, 4 Volumes, London: Routledge.

Spash, C. L. (2011), 'Social Ecological Economics: Understanding the Past to See the Future', *American Journal of Economics and Sociology*, Vol. 70, No. 2, pp. 340–375.

Spash, C. L. (2012), 'New Foundations for Ecological Economics', *Ecological Economics*, Vol. 77, May, pp. 36–47.

Spash, C. L. (2013), 'The Shallow or the Deep Ecological Economics Movement?', *Ecological Economics*, Vol. 93, September, pp. 351–362.

Spash, C. L. (ed.) (2017), *Routledge Handbook of Ecological Economics: Nature and Society*, Abingdon and New York: Routledge.

Spash, C. L. and Ryan, A. (2012), 'Economic Schools of Thought on the Environment: Investigating Unity and Division', *Cambridge Journal of Economics*, Vol. 36, No. 5, pp. 1091–1121.

Epilogue

What is Rethinking Economics and how can you get involved?

Rethinking Economics is an international network of students, academics and professionals building a better economics in society and the classroom. Through a mixture of campaigning, events and engaging projects, Rethinking Economics connects people globally to discuss and enact the change needed to create a brighter future for economics.

This epilogue will give you a quick overview of Rethinking Economics and how you can get involved. For the most up-to-date information, visit our website at www. rethinkeconomics.org. If you have any questions or comments about this book, you can contact the editorial team at *reader@rethinkeconomics.org*.

What do we want

Reform the curriculum

Rethinking Economics was started by students who were unhappy with what they were being taught in their undergraduate economics degrees. So, what's so wrong with the standard economics curriculum?

A Lack of Pluralism Economic perspectives are like maps, which try to explain our economy by simplifying it. They help us understand the world but become dangerous when we forget (as we have today) that they are by definition only partial and incomplete. Recognising that there is a plurality of ways to study the economy is absolutely necessary for a good, quality education.

A Lack of Real-World Application Lectures and tutorials typically deal with abstract theoretical models, and students are rarely, if ever, asked to use real-world data. Students shouldn't graduate with economics degrees without being taught basic facts about the economies in which they live.

A Lack of Critical Thinking Students are expected not to question the models they are presented with in lectures and tutorials. Not only is this bad for students' academic development, but it is poor preparation for the workplace, where professional economists must approach policies and data with a sceptical eye.

Economics for everyone

Economics is a discipline that impacts everyone, yet it is also a subject where few people are able to have their say. While most people want to understand and engage with the economic decisions and events that affect their lives, many also think that the subject is not for them, or is something best left to the 'experts'.

In a time where all our politicians seem to talk about is the economy, this is dangerous for democracy. In a poll of British adults we ran in collaboration with Yougov in 2015, we found that only 12% of respondents found that economics was spoken about in a way that is easy and accessible to understand. Furthermore, we found that only 39% of respondents could define Gross Domestic Product, 43% the Government Budget Deficit and 30% Quantitative Easing. However, when we asked whether people would like to know more about economics, only 13% of respondents said 'no'.

There are real barriers that keep people from interacting with economics. At Rethinking Economics we want to tear down as many of those barriers as possible to create an economics that is both engaging and understandable.

What are we doing?

Local organising is the lifeblood of Rethinking Economics. Students in local RE groups self-educate themselves by putting on events, lobby their departments for curriculum reform, and bring economics as it should be to their communities. As of the time of this writing, there are over 50 member groups in 15 countries, but these numbers seem to grow steadily month after month.

Rethinking Economics also serves as a platform to launch bigger projects – like this book – that involve a much broader network of students, academics and professionals. In the spring of 2016 we launched Economy (www.ecnmy.org), our news and entertainment platform dedicated to promoting 'understandable economics'. And at the end of 2016, we released *The Econocracy*, a book written by Rethinking students about the "perils of leaving economics to the experts" and "the struggle for the soul of economics".

We also work closely with our friends in the International Student Initiative for Pluralism in Economics (ISIPE), a sister group also working to reform economics. Led by the French group (PEPS Économie), ISIPE was able to conduct an expansive survey of economics curriculums around the world to show just how narrow and uniform they really are. The German-speaking network (Netzwerk Plurale Ökonomik) has also created an incredible open-source e-learning platform, called Exploring Economics (www.exploring-economics.org), that presents extensive information about a variety of economic theories, topics and methods in both German and English.

What can you do?

Join the movement! Whether you're a student, an academic, an economics teacher or an interested member of the public, you can become a rethinker. Being a part of Rethinking Economics can be as easy as following our newsletter or adding your name to our manifesto or as involved as starting a local group and helping to actively run the network. We have loads of projects that need helping hands, and we are always eager for people with new ideas.

So check us out at www.rethinkeconomics.org, click the "Become a Rethinker" button, and dare to Rethink Economics.

Index

Note: Page numbers in *italic* indicate a figure on the corresponding page.